The story is told realistically, [...] all four Gospels, with
events as nearly as possible in chronological order. Jesus
himself left no documents or papers but many witnesses
who had watched him heal, seen the feeding of the five
thousand, and heard countless times his message which was
to bring the whole world into that kingdom 'which is not
meat and drink, but righteousness, and peace, and joy in
the Holy Spirit'. These men learned the Lord's Prayer from
his lips, and passed it on so that it has come right down to
our own generation. Of them it is Peter who speaks
through St Mark's Gospel, and through St John's come the
words of the only one among them who remained with
Jesus throughout the night of questioning; the only one
courageous enough to stand by him, at the foot of the
cross, until the end.

THE STORY OF JESUS

BY ELEANOR GRAHAM

ILLUSTRATED BY BRIAN WILDSMITH

PUFFIN BOOKS

PUFFIN BOOKS

Published by the Penguin Group
Penguin Books Ltd, 27 Wrights Lane, London W8 5TZ, England
Penguin Books USA Inc., 375 Hudson Street, New York, New York 10014, USA
Penguin Books Australia Ltd, Ringwood, Victoria, Australia
Penguin Books Canada Ltd, 10 Alcorn Avenue, Toronto, Ontario, Canada M4V 3B2
Penguin Books (NZ) Ltd, 182–190 Wairau Road, Auckland 10, New Zealand

Penguin Books Ltd, Registered Offices: Harmondsworth, Middlesex, England

First published in Puffin Books 1959
Revised edition 1971
Reissued 1993
1 3 5 7 9 10 8 6 4 2

Printed in England by Clays Ltd, St Ives plc
Set in Linotype Juliana

'BUT WHO SHALL BUILD HIM
A HOUSE, WHEN THE HEAVEN
AND THE HEAVEN OF HEAVENS
CANNOT CONTAIN HIM!'

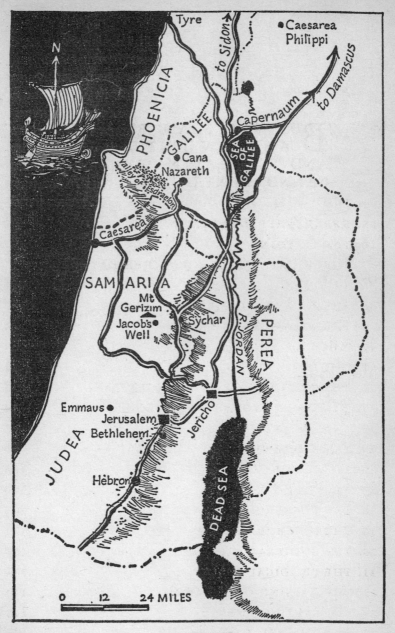

N

Tyre

to Sidon

Caesarea
Philippi

PHOENICIA

GALILEE

Cana

Nazareth

Capernaum

SEA OF GALILEE

to Damascus

Valley of Esdraelon

Caesarea

SAMARIA

Mt
Gerizim

Jacob's
Well

Sychar

R. JORDAN

PEREA

Emmaus

Jerusalem

Bethlehem

Jericho

JUDEA

Hebron

DEAD SEA

0   12   24 MILES

PALESTINE

CONTENTS

Contents

CHAPTER 1

STANDING IN THE PRESENCE
OF GOD

THE people in the outer courts of the Temple were praying as they waited for the priest to come out and speak to them. The hour of sacrifice was over, the smoke of the incense had risen from the altar in the Holy Place. But no one came. Their prayers were broken by inquiring glances towards the steps above them. The delay was unusual, strange. Then at last they saw the old man come out in his robes. He stood looking down at them. They raised their eyes towards him, waiting for the blessing, but none came. The silence was unbroken. He opened his mouth and his face worked as though he was trying to produce words, but no sound came forth.

'He has seen a vision,' someone said.

The old man was moving his head uneasily from side to side. He raised and dropped his arms and walked uncertainly back into the Temple.

Yes, he had had a vision as he waited before the altar of incense with the sweet mixture of gums and resins ready to be burnt. A figure seemed suddenly to be standing near him, just on the right of the altar. With extra care he brought the incense to the fire, and the sweet smoke rose from it, but his hands were shaking.

'Don't be afraid,' said the stranger. 'I have news for you. Elisabeth your wife is going to give you the son you have been praying for. His name will be John.'

'I did pray for a son,' Zacharias thought, 'but ... Elisabeth to have a child now ... when we are both old ...'

'A son who will bring you great happiness,' the stranger

9

was saying. 'There will be rejoicing over his coming into the world. He will lead many people back to God. You will see him grow in the spirit and power of Elijah. The purpose of these things is to prepare our people for the coming of the Lord.'

Zacharias trembled. He had often read the words the

stranger used in the Holy Books where the wisdom of the ancient prophets had been written down.

'How shall I know whether to believe what you have told me?' he asked, getting out the words with difficulty. 'I am an old man, and my wife is old.'

He did not look up, but he heard the stranger say, 'I am Gabriel, standing in the presence of God. I was sent to tell you these things, these good tidings. Let this be the proof. You will be dumb until with your own eyes you see your son. What I have told you, shall come to pass.'

The vision faded. Zacharias remembered his duties, and the people waiting outside, but he forgot that dumbness was to come upon him, and he went out, like a sleepwalker, to give the blessing. He stood there, trying to speak the familiar words, but no sound came.

He went slowly back through the big doors in a daze, Gabriel's words sounding through his head, 'I am Gabriel, standing in the presence of God.' He recalled how the prophet Daniel had once heard a voice call out, 'Gabriel, make this man to understand the vision.'

Dumbness was no great affliction at that moment to Zacharias. His mind was in a turmoil, for he believed what he had heard.

He had several days yet to run of his period of duty in the Temple, during which he did not see his wife. When at length he went home, what he had to tell had to be conveyed in dumb show or in writing.

In due course, Elisabeth discovered that, in spite of her age, she was really going to have a baby, and her heart glowed with happiness, for it was shameful to be childless. She had endured pity and scorn from family and friends for a long time on that account, so now she hid herself until there could be no shadow of doubt, and as every day she grew more certain, she thanked God for so blessing her, and taking that shame from her.

Three months before the time for her baby to be born, Gabriel came again as God's messenger, this time to a young girl who had just been betrothed to a man called Joseph, a carpenter. Though he worked with his hands for his living, he was descended from the great King David. Wars and persecutions and massacres had changed many people's lives, and Joseph had nothing to do with kings or palaces – but he was a good man and a good carpenter. Betrothal in that country was more than an engagement of two people to marry. It was an actual part of the marriage ceremony, and as binding.

To this girl, whose name was Mary, came Gabriel and said, 'Hail Mary, the Lord is with you! Blessed are you above all women.'

Mary was startled to see a strange man standing beside her in the house, and his greeting puzzled her.

'Don't be afraid,' Gabriel said, 'it is from God I come. He has chosen you for a special purpose. You are to be the mother of a boy who will be known as the Son of the Most High. He will be great. David's throne will be given him, and he shall reign for ever. Of the kingdom over which he will reign, there shall be no end. You will call him Jesus because that name means "Saviour".'

'I don't understand,' Mary said slowly, 'I am not yet married.'

'What will happen will be a holy thing,' said Gabriel. 'The spirit of God will come upon you, and His shadow will pass over you. Don't be afraid. Your cousin Elisabeth, who is old, is also going to have a child. This is the sixth month with her though it was thought impossible for her to have a child now.'

Mary bowed her head in great humility.

'I am the handmaid of the Lord,' she replied simply. 'What His will is, I will do.' And the angel left her.

For Elisabeth, Gabriel's message had been the cause of great rejoicing. For Mary, it was not so simple. Joseph was good and kind, but it was a strange story she had to tell him. Would he believe it, and protect her? Would their marriage go on? Or would he reject her, and inflict on her the awful disgrace of divorce? Disgrace . . . or even death by stoning?

In her perplexity and anxiety, the thought of her old cousin Elisabeth kept coming into her mind, and at last she resolved to visit her.

Elisabeth and Zacharias lived in a little town in the hills a few miles out of Jerusalem. Mary went there on foot, and as she reached their door, Elisabeth came out to greet her, and suddenly pressed a hand over her heart.

'At the sound of your voice, my baby leapt inside me,' she said. It had felt as though fire had run through her. She looked into Mary's eyes and read her secret, then in a voice of ecstasy she cried, 'Blessed are you, O Mary, of all women, and blessed your child. It's wonderful when people trust the word of God. I am honoured that the mother of my Lord has come to visit me.'

Elisabeth's words, echoing what Gabriel had said, soothed Mary's troubled mind. All anxiety dropped from her, and she crossed her hands on her breast, and said:

'My soul doth magnify the Lord, and my spirit hath rejoiced in God my Saviour, for he hath condescended to the lowliness of his handmaiden.'

She stayed there in Zacharias's home until almost the time for Elisabeth's child to be born. Indeed it came almost as soon as she had left, and was a fine boy. Friends and neighbours of the family came dropping in to see mother and baby, congratulated Elisabeth warmly and admired the child.

Zacharias had been dumb all this time. It was not until eight days after the baby was born that he got his speech back. Guests were assembled for the boy's circumcision, and everyone was asking what he was to be called. Elisabeth told them, John, and there was a great outcry at that. Relations were all exclaiming:

'Nobody in this family is called John! He ought to be Zacharias after his father.'

They sent a servant to fetch Zacharias, who was already on his way from the Temple bringing his wax tablets with him as usual. He listened to the women all speaking at once, and then he began to write on the tablet, 'His name must be John'. But before he had got half through it, he found he could speak and finished the sentence aloud, then raised his voice in words of thanksgiving to God for his great goodness.

The guests began to glance at one another wonderingly. It was strange for the old priest to get his speech back suddenly like this. It was almost as extraordinary as his wife's having a baby so late in life. There was something unusual too about their happiness. They looked at the baby as though he was something from another world. So a little awe crept into the room. They heard Zacharias raise a hymn of praise as he stood looking down at his son, thinking also of the other child that was to come into the world.

'Blessed be the Lord God of Israel,' he chanted, and his old voice grew strong and steady as the words rang out, 'for he hath visited and redeemed his people, and hath raised up a mighty salvation for us in the house of his servant, David. And thou, child, shalt be called the prophet of the Highest, for thou shalt go before the face of the Lord to prepare His ways, to give knowledge of salvation to His people for the remission of their sins.'

In the meantime Mary went home and told Joseph about the coming child. He was greatly distressed as she had expected, and for some days she did not know what he was going to do. He was kind and would not want her to suffer, as she was bound to suffer if he divorced her. Yet that was what the Law required. He began to wonder if he could arrange matters quietly, sending Mary away secretly so that no one would know what had happened.

One night he fell into a deep sleep from which he woke suddenly sure what he ought to do. He was at peace again, and there was contentment in his heart. Echoing through his head were the words, 'Take courage, Joseph. Marry Mary. What is wrought in her is of God.'

He lay still in the darkness, repeating to himself, 'What is wrought in her is of God.' The baby is there by the will of God. Now, like Mary, he could say humbly and thankfully, 'God's will be done!' – and fear no more.

He went on thinking for a while about his being a son of David. Nothing could change that, though no one thought of him, the hard-working carpenter, as anything but the plain man he was, who made the things they needed for their houses and their work.

He remembered what Mary had said about the angel telling her that her son would mount the throne of David, and at that he cried humbly, 'Blessed be the Name of the Lord!' and left the mysteries in His hands.

Then for Joseph there was no puzzle left, no more anxiety, and he fell into a sound refreshing sleep. He loved Mary and he was going to marry her. He would take care of her, and watch over her like a father. He could not understand what these strange things meant, but he had faith. He trusted God and was not only content, but deeply happy that God should so use him.

Every morning, noon, and sunset, like every good Jew, he repeated the words of the shema.

'*Hear, O Israel, the Lord our God is one, and thou shalt love the Lord thy God with all thy heart, with all thy soul, and with all thy might.*'

CHAPTER 2

BETHLEHEM

GABRIEL had said that the throne of David would belong to Mary's son, but there was already a King of the Jews, though he was no Jew. It was Herod the Great, whose family had been forced to accept that faith a century earlier when their country, Edom, had been conquered by the Jews. Forty years later the Romans conquered Jerusalem, and Herod's father offered his services to the winning side. That was in the time of Julius Caesar, eight years before he first came to Britain (in 55 B.C.).

The Romans found the older Herod useful and put him in charge of practically the whole country. His son, Herod the Great, was educated on Roman lines. He was good-looking and amusing. When he was sixteen he met Mark Antony in Jerusalem, and it was Antony who suggested, some years later when Augustus had succeeded Julius Caesar, that it might be a good move to give the Jews a king who was accepted by them as a Jew though having no feelings of loyalty towards them.

Later, Herod rewarded him with the revenue from the famous gardens of Jericho which Mark Antony gave to Cleopatra.

Israel was very much an 'occupied' country, and had lost most of the rights of government. About this time the Romans called for a proper record of every member of the Jewish population in order to fix taxes, and as many spent their lives wandering up and down the country with their flocks, everyone was ordered to go to the place where his family belonged, and to remain there until the registration was completed.

As Joseph was descended from King David, he had to go to the place where the House of David belonged, and that was Bethlehem. Mary need not have gone, and it was almost time for her baby to be born, but Joseph saddled the donkey and they set out for Bethlehem, he walking beside her all the way. The weather was probably much like our own in December, sometimes wet, often snowy in the hills.

So, Mary and Joseph came to Bethlehem, meeting and passing many other families from all over Israel, all making their way to the places where they belonged.

Bethlehem was crowded when they arrived, for in the course of centuries many descendants had been born to the House of David. There was no room for Mary in the inn, but next to it stood a stable which was free to all. There she could rest beside their donkey, among animals belonging to other travellers. The stable was a great cave, almost dark but for the brightness of the stars which shone through a hole in the roof.

Mary was glad to rest, and in the night her baby was born, and was a son as she had expected. She wrapped him up warmly and laid him in a cattle trough.

A few miles away, out in the snowy hills, there were shepherds keeping watch over their flocks. They had lit a fire to keep away wolves and the flames leapt up brightly, making a circle of light beyond which the darkness closed in like a wall of black glass. The men brought out their food, and ate and talked a little, and fell silent, listening to the howling of wild beasts and staring into the fire. Suddenly, there seemed to be a light out in the darkness. It spread and strengthened as they stared at it, and an angel seemed to be standing in its radiance.

'Don't be afraid,' he said, just as Gabriel had said to Zacharias and to Mary. 'Have no fear. I have come to bring good news – tidings of great joy for you and for all men.'

Then he spoke the words of the prophet Isaiah, which were centuries old:

'For unto you is born this day in the city of David a saviour which is Christ the Lord.' And he went on, 'You will know him by this: the baby lies in a manger, in the food trough in a stable, wrapped in swaddling clothes.'

As he stopped speaking, a crowd of angels seemed to surround him, singing, and the words the shepherds heard were, 'Glory to God in the Highest, peace on earth, good will among men.'

The light faded as though many lamps had gone out, and the shepherds were alone again under a sky full of stars, and their fire no longer seemed so big and bright. They were not frightened any more, but breathless. They scrambled to their feet, muttering broken words, repeating snatches of what the angel had said. Then, calling to each other and to their sheep, they turned towards Bethlehem in search of the baby. They brought their flocks with them. If they had left them alone on the hillside, wolves would soon have made a meal of them. Shepherds and sheep seemed to move quickly, as though their feet knew the way they had to go. Then the men began to look right and left for the stable, and their feet seemed to stop of themselves before the one beside the inn. They went inside, feeling bashful, wondering suddenly what to say if they found a mother there with a baby in a manger. But they did not hesitate. They saw the trough at once, with the mother standing beside it and Joseph near by. The child was awake and his eyes were open. The shepherds shuffled to a stop. What they had heard was true! They had seen a vision, a wonder ... they did not know what to call it ... but it filled them again with exultation, as it had out on the dark hillside.

Something strange and wonderful had happened, and they were there at the heart of it, specially chosen, sent by a host of angels. They had been the first to hear the news. They got awkwardly down on their knees and pulled off their caps, staring, but finding nothing to say. Then they rose and backed out.

Outside in the street, they felt like shouting. They wanted to tell everyone what had happened.

To Mary and Joseph, the shepherds' coming out of the night with their mumbled words about angels and tidings of great joy, and a baby born in a stable, was something else to set beside the Angel Gabriel's visit, and Joseph's message that what was wrought in her was of God. And they had knelt before her baby as though he were a Prince in a Palace instead of lying humbly in a stable. But was his birth to be made known and talked about? Mary understood that he was not just her baby but she was anxious. The shepherds had *knelt* before her baby. They had been brought there on purpose to see the child. Why should humble working men kneel before people so lowly that their baby was born out in a cattle-shed?

When he was eight days old the baby was circumcised, as all Jewish boys were, in token of the ancient bond between God and His people, and he was given the name of Jesus. Many people came to look at him, for the shepherds had talked, and their story had roused curiosity.

Then came three wise men from the East, men who studied the stars. It happened that each of them, in their distant countries, had read the same news from the sky, and took it to mean that a great Prince had been born who would make the whole world free.

They set out separately, but after a time the roads by which the star had led them, met, and when each had told his news, they found they were all going the same way, and they travelled on together. It was to Israel the stars had pointed as the home of the Prince, so they were making for Jerusalem, expecting to find him there, in the Palace of the King of the Jews.

They were well received. King Herod saw them himself and invited them to tell him why they had come. Though he had four grown-up sons, there was no infant prince in his Palace. He was a sick man and near the end of his days. He had enjoyed power, and the thought that he must die and someone else inherit all he possessed sent him into uncontrollable rages. The wise men's story of a new-born Prince put him into a terrifying rage, for fear someone was plotting against him. He knew most people would be glad to be rid of him.

What could this story of a Prince mean? Though he did not believe in the Jewish faith, he had heard of the 'Deliverer' they expected to come. Was he expected to deliver them from himself? And was that who had been born? Herod was not of royal blood. He had not been born to be King. Some quite low born child might be going to succeed him.

He hid his rage from the three wise men, and invited them to wait while he obtained information for them. They were taken to a room where food and drink were brought, while he sent for the High Priest and some of the Elders.

It was a rude summons, and offended the Priests who were also proud and arrogant, but when he called, they had to obey.

Herod asked at once where they expected their Messiah to be born: and they told him, in Bethlehem, the City of David. That was enough; he dismissed them, and told the wise men to go on to Bethlehem.

'When you have found the child,' he added, 'return and let me know, for I too should like to go and pay homage.'

The three men bowed and took their leave, and now a star seemed to lead them down the Hebron road. Their fine camels swayed and swung along it and, each in his own way, thought of what they had seen while Herod was speaking, how different the light in his eyes had been from his words.

'I trust him not,' each was saying in his heart, 'I trust him not.'

The camels bore them on to Bethlehem, to the inn, and it seemed that the star which had sent them out on this long journey, and had led them to Jerusalem, now came to rest over the stable beside the inn. The camels sank on their knees for their masters to alight, and the wise men went in and saw the child: and Mary and Joseph drew closer to him protectingly.

The wise men had no doubt about this being the child they sought. There seemed to be a radiance about him, and each after the custom of his country made deep obeisance. Then they went to their saddle-bags, and each brought out his greatest treasure. Spending so much of their lives on the old caravan routes where merchants were constantly passing with rich cargoes and precious ware, it was convenient to have something worth trading; now they brought out for the child their best – gold and frankincense and myrrh.

The wise men's voices sounded strange to Mary and Joseph, yet it seemed that they too spoke of the child as a great King-to-be, whose coming was to save the world.

As she had watched the shepherds go clumsily through the rough rocky archway, now Mary let these men from their distant lands go, searching their faces for any clue to what life was going to bring to her child. She watched them lead their camels out and disappear into the darkness.

There was mystery upon mystery connected with the child and she was troubled, though not afraid. Very quietly she gathered him to her, holding him warmly and comfortingly.

As the camels got into their stride, the three wise men turned their heads away from Jerusalem and Herod's Palace, and returned to their homes by other paths.

It did not take Herod long to realize that they had disregarded him. The Palace echoed with his wrath. He was determined that the young Prince should not escape him. If necessary he would kill every child born within the last month – or the last year – or two years – in or around Bethlehem. That ought to settle the question.

That night Joseph woke suddenly, hearing in a dream the awful echo of Herod's words, and a voice which seemed to be urgently telling him to get up.

'Take Mary and the child away from this place,' it said. 'Go down into Egypt, and remain there until it is safe to return.'

Joseph did not hesitate. He got up and rolled their few possessions into a bundle, with the gifts of the wise men inside it. He untied the donkey, roused Mary, and lifted the child out of the manger. So, in the night, the little family went quietly away to travel the many miles to Egypt, keeping away from the good roads to avoid Herod's men and Roman soldiers. Mary, on the donkey, with Jesus held warmly against her, looked out into the darkness, still the handmaid of the Lord, accepting His will, but not understanding it.

A day or two after they had gone, Herod's orders went out for all children under two years old in Bethlehem and round about to be killed. Soldiers marched in and carried out the order, and there were perhaps fifty babies killed that day.

CHAPTER 3

AT HOME IN NAZARETH

ABOUT three months later Joseph heard that Herod was dead, and left Egypt to return with his family along the road that went through Bethlehem and on to Jerusalem. Day after day they journeyed on, and at night slept in the open beside other travellers coming and going by the same road.

One night as he lay looking up into the sky, with only the occasional fall of ashes as the camp fire died down, or the distant cry of a jackal to break the silence, he found his anxiety fading, and a plan forming clearly in his mind. He would not go near Bethlehem or Jerusalem, but to Galilee where he was well known. He would take by-paths to avoid meeting people. In Nazareth he would get out his tools and would soon be busy again, making ploughs, and yokes for oxen, tables and stools and all the other things people needed for their homes and work.

He led the donkey off the road next day, along a track through the hills where they met only flocks and shepherds. A few more days and they were crossing a great plain, and starting up the rocky path to the little town of Nazareth with its white flat-topped houses rising up the slope.

It was spring, and the days were warm with a light, pleasant breeze. The fields were bright with flowers, and between the houses grew scrubby black-twigged fig trees, silvery-grey olives, and an occasional cypress. Sometimes a small vineyard was squeezed between two walls, sometimes great boulders of bare rock rose up above the roofs. Precipitous cliffs fell away from the little town starkly. Above, the hill rose steeply another five hundred feet.

Joseph knew every inch of the way, and smiled down at the sleeping baby as he remembered how the village boys used to play over the housetops, running out of one door on to the roof of the house below, racing down the steps which ran outside the houses from the roof to the ground.

Nazareth was small, but there was always plenty going on, for the caravan road to Damascus passed through it, and men of many nations stopped at the well for water.

Joseph had always liked to climb to the top of the hill and look out over the country, to the Sea of Galilee to the east, a great lovely lake with a snow-capped mountain rising up on its far side. To the west lay the Mediterranean, and north-ward, Syria and the mountains and forests of Lebanon – but in the south Jerusalem stood, girded about by the high red hills of Judea. It was the south that always held his eyes longest, and he would repeat softly, 'I will lift up mine eyes unto the hills, whence cometh my help' – and 'If I forget thee, O Jerusalem, let my right hand lose her cunning!' – and it was his right hand that wielded the saw and plane and hammer, and earned their living.

Southwards too, but nearer home, lay the great Plain of Esdraelon, scene of some of the most terrible battles of the past. Gideon had put out the fleece there at night, to know if God was with him. David had so heavily defeated the Philistines, that his musicians sang that Saul slew his thousands, but David his tens of thousands.

So, Joseph and Mary came to Nazareth and made their home there. Joseph laid in wood for his work. Mary unpacked the mats and rugs to cover the rock floor in their main room, brought out the little hand mill to grind corn for bread, the cooking pots, bowls and plates. She probably had to buy the great earthenware jars for fetching water from the well, and there was only one well at Nazareth, then and always, right up to a few years ago. She had a lamp to buy too, and oil.

Joseph made stools and a table, a stand for the lamp, perhaps
a manger for the donkey's food.

In this humble home Jesus grew to boyhood, knowing from
his earliest days the good smell of wood, watching the trickle
of sawdust as it fell from the saw and the wood shavings as
they floated down from the plane. He learned the ordinary

things of childhood, to crawl and to stand, to scramble up and
down steps, to walk and run, to feed and dress himself, to talk
and to listen, to know the happiness of being loved and himself loving and giving.

Every Friday he saw Joseph put away his tools and sweep
up the chips and sawdust, to be ready for the Sabbath to
begin at six o-clock. Mary too finished her work early and
had food prepared for the next day. At six o'clock she lit the
little lamp (so often called a 'candle' in the Bible).

The Jews were gentle with their children, and handed on to them early the story of their special relationship to God. Jesus would certainly have listened to the ancient story of the creation, of the first man and woman in the Garden of Eden, and how the animals got their names. He soon knew the story of Noah and the ark. But when he came to the story of Abraham, it was history he was learning, the history of the beginnings of the Jewish people. He heard about Joseph and his coat of many colours and that it was through him that those early Hebrews came to be Pharaoh's slaves, as God had warned Abraham, and that it was Moses who freed them. Perhaps Mary told him, 'We took you to Egypt when you were a baby, but we were free and soon came away again.'

It was Joseph's duty to teach him, first the *Shema* which, thereafter, Jesus said night and morning every day of his life, as all good Jews did.

'Hear, O Israel, the Lord our God is one. And thou shalt love the Lord thy God with all thy heart, with all thy soul, and with all thy might.'

Joseph taught him too about the great festivals of the year and what each meant, and that the most important was the Passover, in memory of their being saved from that terrible time of slavery in Egypt. The story of Moses came to Jesus a little differently, told in connection with this feast, and he saw many downtrodden people waiting in their dark huts that night with the blood of a kid smeared on their doors, waiting to know if Moses had succeeded, if it was to be freedom, or an even harder slavery. Passover was kept at lambing time, when we keep Easter. Fifty days later there was Pentecost, when the corn was ripening, it was the Season of First Fruits. In autumn came the feast of Tabernacles, and a few days before our Christmas, the feast of Dedication.

Every Jew went to Jerusalem for the Passover if he possibly could, even those who had left Israel and were living abroad in Syria, Greece, Egypt, or elsewhere. Jesus learned that he would go too when he was twelve, and would travel there with bands of other pilgrims, singing psalms and raising their voices together in prayer as they walked the hilly miles. After that, he would be reckoned a man, though he would still have to go to school. He would be presented in the Synagogue by Joseph, and could fight for his country if need be.

Joseph also told him of the Covenants God had made with man, with Noah after the flood, then with Abraham, and with Moses. Perhaps he told him also of the new Covenant Jeremiah had foreseen, when the word of God would lie so deeply in a man's heart that he would know it of himself, without having to be taught by other men. Probably he added too what he knew of the promise of a Messiah who was to show the whole world a new righteousness.

There was a Synagogue at Nazareth, perhaps only a room in some house, but kept strictly as a Sanctuary to which people could go for the comfort of hearing the Scriptures read and expounded, to pray together and to bless the Name of the Lord. There were no priests attached to Synagogues; sacrifices were only made in the Temple at Jerusalem. There was a council of Elders, and one man was chosen to arrange all the Synagogue affairs. Each Synagogue kept a school for boys between the ages of six and sixteen, and attendance was compulsory for them, but girls need not go unless their parents wished it. In Jesus' time the Synagogues were also Courts of a kind to which wrongdoers could be summoned, and punished.

Service was held in the Synagogue every Sabbath morning, and Jesus probably first went when he was about three, carefully washed, and dressed in fresh clothes, as a small way of doing honour to God when going to visit Him in His house. He was warned by Mary that there would be no figs to nibble, and he must not whisper or talk aloud during the service. In God's house, thoughts must be all of God, for a child has to learn how to love God.

A small place like Nazareth would not possess many books in those days when all books had to be written by hand. But there was certainly a copy of the book of Isaiah, almost certainly one of the Psalms, and probably the five scrolls of the books of the Law.

At Nazareth there was certainly a copy of the book of Isaiah, almost certainly one of the Psalms, and probably the five scrolls of the books of the Law. Rich men might possess scrolls of their own and bring them to the Synagogue from time to time, and passing scholars or other learned men sometimes carried one with them, and brought it to the Synagogue where anyone who liked could go and hear it read.

CHAPTER 4

THOU SHALT – AND SHALT NOT

JESUS went to school when he was six like any other Jewish boy. Rich people had tutors for their children but Joseph and Mary were poor and Jesus went to the village school in the Synagogue.

The first lesson for all children was to learn the ten commandments. Then they were copied from the Scroll on to wax tablets with a little sharp-pointed stick. That meant being able to read the words as well as writing them, and as they were in ancient Hebrew (which was not spoken in everyday life), the boys learned their old language as they went along.

The ten commandments are those we still learn today.

1. Love God, and take to yourselves no other gods.
2. Do not make for yourselves idols like the golden calf, do not worship the sun or the moon, do not make offerings to the sea.
3. Beware of swearing falsely in God's name.
4. You have six days in which to work. Do all you have to do in them, and keep the seventh day free for God.
5. Honour your parents.
6. Do not kill: life is sacred.
7. Do not commit adultery: marriage is sacred.
8. Do not steal.
9. Do not lie to or about one another.
10. Do not cheat your neighbour, and do not thirst for those things which are his.

When the boys knew these commandments thoroughly, they went on to the book of Leviticus to learn the instructions given there about the ritual in the Temple and the sacrifices which each of them would have to make in time. They learned as well the matters of hygiene, about leprosy, and the order that no leper could be considered cured until he had shown himself to a priest and been declared clean.

At school the children sat on the floor round their teacher, and learned by repeating together after him a phrase at a time. Their writing was carefully watched, because the Elders of the Synagogue were always looking for boys to be trained as scribes, and there were special schools for them. Jesus does not seem to have been so singled out, but probably even as a small boy he was more interested in what the words meant than in merely copying them. Schools had been started long ago when people were afraid that all their books might one day be destroyed by enemies. If every child was taught the important parts, the books themselves would matter less, for the substance could be handed on by word of mouth from one to another.

Thus the Law was taught first, and then the writings of the Prophets which held so much of truth and wisdom. The

Prophets had had that extra sense which gives insight and makes men sensitive to the hand of God and to His messages. They were all great men, but Elijah was considered the greatest. Isaiah had wonderful vision, and deep understanding, but Moses was not only a prophet, but the great Law-giver, and the hero who had freed the Hebrews from slavery in Egypt.

So all the children's education turned on 'the Law and the Prophets'. They could only study at school the Scrolls which their Synagogue possessed, but in Jerusalem there were copies of all the Scriptures, and in the courts of the Temple the most learned scholars in the land taught from them openly for anyone who cared to listen, even children. Jerusalem promised all the things the teacher could not tell, and in the spring after his twelfth birthday Jesus would be going there for the Passover.

As the time for the pilgrimage to Jerusalem drew near, people in Nazareth made up parties for the journey and all travelled together, for it was a long way to go on foot. The older people trudged along at a steady pace, but the young ones raced forward, or loitered and rested until they got left

behind, then came rushing on again pell-mell. The straggling crowd grew as each small path brought more to join it.

It was early spring, with soft breezes and warm sunshine. The fields were bright with flowers, purple, white and yellow, scarlet, and brilliant blue, with feathery tamarisks blooming everywhere. When they crossed the Plain of Esdraelon, the first green shoots were coming up in the great cornfields which stretched away and away on either hand.

The men who headed the procession sang as they marched slowly on. There were special Psalms which belonged to this Passover journey to Jerusalem. All the bands of pilgrims were singing them, and sometimes the sound from those on other roads echoed across and men half turned their heads to listen.

Jesus knew the Pilgrimage Psalms, the 84th and the sequence from the 121st to the 134th, and with all his heart he sang, 'I was glad when they said unto me, Let us go into the house of the Lord. Our feet shall stand within thy gates, O Jerusalem. Jerusalem is built as a city that is compact, whither the tribes go up to give thanks.' That was really Jerusalem, a city 'compact', tightly packed within its high walls, set on the topmost slope of its hills, aslant, facing towards the East. In Jerusalem he would go to the great teachers and his questions would be answered. He would hear the word of the Lord. 'As the mountains are round about Jerusalem,' he sang, 'so the Lord is round about his people.'

They sang also, 'Lord, remember David and all his afflictions. How he sware unto the Lord, "Surely I will not come within the tabernacle of my house, nor go up into my bed. I will not give sleep to mine eyes nor slumber to mine eyelids, until I find out a place for the Temple of the Lord!"'

Yet it was not David who built the first Temple, but Solomon, who had cried in humility of spirit, 'How shall I build Him a house, when the heaven and the heaven of heavens *cannot contain him?'* It was not Solomon's Temple Jesus was going to see, nor even the one that was built again on the ruins of the first, however, but a third which Herod meant to outshine even Solomon's in magnificence, but it was still unfinished.

As they drew near Jerusalem the pilgrims split up into parties of between ten and twenty people, each led by the father or one chosen to take his place. Each party would have its Paschal lamb which was the chief part of the Feast, and had to be eaten entirely at the one meal.

Joseph gathered his family and friends about him, and gave them instructions. He chose their camping site outside the city and left Mary and the other women there to make everything ready. Jesus went with him into Jerusalem, to buy the lamb and to make their offerings in the Temple. The narrow streets were crowded and Jesus saw Roman soldiers standing about, on the watch for trouble. They looked powerful with the authority of Rome behind them, and smiled contemptuously at Jews who fell on their knees and kissed the ground for joy at being in their Holy place.

Joseph and Jesus went into the precincts of the Temple, crossed the wide Court of Gentiles and entered a grand colonnade with shops and booths which Herod had built over the towering eastern wall. But where was the peace and the 'beauty of holiness'? The place was a cattle market. Drovers shouted, and their beasts were driven to and fro; shrill voices were raised in bargaining; sheep were bleating, money changers called out the rate of shekels for Roman money. The coins Rome supplied were engraved with the Emperor's head, so could not be used in the Temple, and pilgrims had to change their money before the sacrifice could be paid for.

Joseph led Jesus through the turmoil and chose their lamb. They took it to a priest to be passed as perfect and without blemish. It was led off and killed, special parts of it being burnt on the great altar. The rest Joseph took back to Mary to be dressed and made ready for the feast.

Also in the Colonnade among all the trafficking with beasts, stood a Synagogue, and the meeting-place of the Sanhedrin, which was the Great Council of Temple Priests and Elders. Joseph pointed them out, but was too occupied with the business in hand for more. They had much to do, he and Jesus, and no time to waste. There was no opportunity then to go in search of the teaching Rabbis, though Jesus saw several groups of men and boys gathered in the courts.

Every moment up to the eating of the feast Jesus was kept busy, as the round of ritual and preparation proceeded, but it was a blessed thing to be eating their Passover in Jerusalem. The lamb was roasted, and bitter herbs such as endive accompanied it in memory of the bitterness of slavery. There were four cups of wine to be passed round. When Joseph as father blessed the first and passed it on, a little ceremony took place. Jesus, as the youngest present, asked the meaning of the feast, then Joseph recited the story of the suffering of their forefathers in Egypt and their liberation by Moses. Special Psalms were sung, three at the beginning – Psalms 113, 114, 115 – and three at the end, 116, 117, 118.

The lamb was eaten, the wine was drunk, and everyone was gay and happy.

Then, almost at once, everything was turmoil again, and they were packing up and getting ready to return. Was this all the visit to Jerusalem was to mean? Was Jesus to go back to Galilee without once having reached the teachers in the Temple? With so much to ask, so much to learn?

On the last morning when everyone was busy, and there was nothing more for Jesus to do, he ran back into the city to snatch that last chance of hearing the things he needed to learn. He found a group of people in the Temple, and worked his way between the men and boys to the front, listening eagerly to all that was going on. It was a discourse intended to stimulate and test the young. Texts were quoted challengingly. An engaging 'What think *you*?' encouraged the timid to speak. This was meat and drink to Jesus. He got his bearings, and pressed forward. His eyes began to sparkle as answers and more questions trembled on his lips. The Rabbis were delighted and began to probe him, testing the quality of his mind, and the extent of his knowledge. Jesus stayed there all day, knowing only that this was what he had expected of Jerusalem, this was what he had been brought there for. Night came and he had no thought for Joseph and Mary. He found some corner of the city to shelter in overnight, and next morning was back in the Court, early, waiting for the master to appear.

Meanwhile, the pilgrims had set out for home, those for Nazareth taking the shorter road over the hills. Neither Joseph nor Mary wondered where Jesus was, they took it for granted that he was with other boys somewhere ahead. It was not until they had made their camp for the night and were having supper that Mary became anxious as Jesus did not come for his share. When the meal was over and he still had not appeared, she grew frightened, for there was always a fear at the back of her mind that something might happen to him. She ran from one campfire to another, asking if anyone knew where he was, Joseph helped her, but at last they saw that Jesus was not with them. What had happened? Had he offended some Roman soldier? Could anyone have connected him with Bethlehem and that massacre of the children?

Quietly Mary and Joseph separated their belongings from those of the rest of the caravan, and went fearfully back to Jerusalem, dreading what they might find.

Joseph knew how the Temple had drawn Jesus, and it was there they went first, and of course there they found him, standing up bright-eyed and flushed in a promising disputation with a Rabbi.

'Son!' Mary cried. 'Why have you treated us like this? You

knew we were returning, and we'd gone a whole day's journey before we missed you! We've been so worried for fear something had happened to you.'

To Jesus her words were surprising. The thing he had found for himself in the Temple seemed to him the most important and the most natural thing in the world for him to be doing. Hadn't she really known what had been so deeply in his mind?

'Didn't you know I should be in my Father's house?' he asked wonderingly, and the way he said it silenced her. This was another of the moments she always remembered and brooded over. He went with them dutifully, leaving Jerusalem with all its promises, and trudged the long miles back to Nazareth, and there he remained until he grew to manhood.

CHAPTER 5

REPENT! REPENT! REPENT!

ELISABETH and Zacharias brought up their son as they had been told to, teaching him the discipline that would make him able to live like Elijah, as a hermit, learning strength through self-denial. His education was different from that of Jesus because John was a priest's son. He had greater opportunities for study and more Scrolls were available for him from the first, but all he learned still depended on the Law and the Prophets.

He did not serve as a priest like his father. It is thought that his parents died before he grew up, for they were old when he was born, but they started him off on the right lines so that he accepted his hard life, recognizing that he had a task to accomplish.

John too learned much of the Scriptures by heart and out in the wildness of the country he could look at them, as it were, in God's presence, seeking for light on the work he had to do.

He ate what he found growing wild, and drank from springs, but often went hungry, and the fasting helped him to feel God's presence and taught him strength of purpose.

His father had told him about the strange vision of the angel Gabriel by the Incense Altar, and how he had been born in the old age of his parents so that a work of God should be accomplished. Zacharias would have failed in his duty if he had not tried to convey all he knew of what that work might mean, and what he knew came from the words of the Prophets about the coming of the Messiah.

John knew that he was to prepare the people for the coming of the Lord, but he had yet to discover how that was to be done. He had been taught that he should 'walk in the spirit and power of Elijah', but he knew that could not mean just living in a cave, wearing a hair shirt and living austerely. He had learned the words which close the Old Testament, at the end of the book of Malachi. '*Behold, I will send you Elijah the prophet before the coming of the great and dreadful day of the Lord; and he shall turn the hearts of the fathers to the children, and the hearts of the children to their fathers.*'

That was part of what Gabriel had told Zacharias that day in the Temple. 'The great and dreadful day of the Lord' suggested terrible things to John, as it had to his father: God angry and sending death and destruction to the earth with fire and brimstone. That idea inspired him, but hindered him too, for those were ideas of the past, and not of what was to come. In the meantime, he prepared himself to go out, and to be on the watch for some sign which would tell him of the coming of the Messiah.

He believed too in Malachi's message of comfort, '*I am the Lord, and I change not. Return to me and I will return to you.*'

When Malachi lived, the country had swarmed with robbers and brigands. They hid in the hills and swooped down on travellers who looked worth robbing. So important men sent 'forerunners' before they went on a journey, to deal with the robbers and make the road safe.

John saw himself as someone of that kind, going ahead and clearing the road for the coming of the Messiah, but he knew a strong arm and stout stick would not be much use to him. His task was not to drive bad people away, but to gather them in, repentant and ready to turn over a new leaf in time to greet the Coming One. John had no doubt that it was the Messiah who was to come. But in spite of the writings of the Prophets, and their clear warnings, no one knew what that Coming would mean.

John understood that the coming of the Messiah was something that belonged to the world of the spirit. The kingdom of Heaven, in words that were later written to the Romans, is not meat and drink, but righteousness, and peace, and joy in the Holy Spirit. It must in some way start inside you, making you want to find God of your own free will.

The first thing was to rouse people, to stir them till they burned with eagerness to hear God's word, with desire to live according to His will. And John had lived very near to God out on the hills, with nothing to distract him but wind and rain, and the cries of the birds and beasts, but his work was with people. He had to keep the ordinary lives of men before him as he listened for the voice of God. But in spite of living like a hermit John was essentially a practical man. He knew men and understood how their minds worked, he could follow their thoughts.

He recognized that it would never be enough just to make them stop and listen. They would have to stay and talk honestly about themselves and he must know how to help them.

A day came when he had to leave his cave and go back into the world. Perhaps the One who was to come was already on his way, might even be near at hand, unrecognized, unsuspected. But it was not for John to go in search of him. For all he knew, they might never meet. But if they did, John was sure he would know him. Galilee was so far from John's haunts that he probably had never seen Jesus, and knew no reason to connect him with his own destiny.

So, John left the wilds and came to the cities, and took his stand at busy cross roads where there were always people coming and going. He chose the Jericho road which runs down from Jerusalem, across the Jordan to Damascus. It was the last road that Elijah had trodden. There John took his stand, a bronzed, hairy figure in a hermit's coat, and his strong voice rang out, crying, 'Repent! Repent! Think again! – for the Kingdom of Heaven is at hand.'

41

Many people stopped to listen, some serious, others curious, many just taking the chance to rest for a moment on their journey.

People who stayed to talk, found themselves being led through an examination of the way they lived. If they stayed long enough, they reached real repentance, and with it a longing for a new and better life. Those who got so far were led down to the Jordan, which was shallow at that place, and baptized.

The Jews already had a sort of baptism, but not for themselves, only for the admission of Gentiles to Judaism. What was strange was that John was baptizing people who had been born Jews and had never abandoned their faith though they had neglected it. He made it a sign of spiritual cleansing and renewal, a making ready for salvation, and he cried, 'I baptize you with water, unto repentance, repent – and quickly, for time is flying! But he who comes after me will baptize with the fire of the spirit. He is the mighty one – I am not worthy even to untie his shoes. He will take his fan in hand and clear his threshing floor thoroughly. He will bestow the wheat in his barns, but will throw the chaff on unquenchable fire. The axe of the woodman also is laid to the roots of the trees. Those that bear no fruit will he hew down, casting them as dead wood on the fire.'

When Roman soldiers stopped to poke fun at him, and asked satirically, 'What about us, Prophet? What do we do to show your *fruits of repentance?*' John looked them in the eye and gave them the straight answer.

'Don't use violence unnecessarily. Don't make false charges against innocent people. Be satisfied with your pay.'

Once some well-to-do travellers paused to inquire what he would like them to do, and he told them, 'You have two coats. Give one to those who have none. You have plenty to eat. Give some of your plenty to those who are hungry.'

One day a group of tax gatherers stopped and put the same question. Tax gatherers were Jews who worked voluntarily for the Romans, and were therefore regarded as worse than traitors. The Romans did not assess each person separately on what he possessed for these taxes, but simply told them to collect a certain amount of money altogether, anything they managed to extract over and above that sum, they could keep. They got no other pay – but many of them grew rich.

To these men John replied, 'Take only what your masters expect.'

As the travellers continued on their way, there was naturally a good deal of talk about the Prophet down by the Jericho road. News of him soon reached the Priests and Elders in the Temple and they, being responsible for what was taught throughout the country, sent a deputation to find out more about him.

John stood in no awe of the Temple. He had heard too much about it from his father, and had known many of the priests and Rabbis all his life.

The deputation took in his hermit's coat, and stood aside, watching him coolly.

'What, you here?' John shouted, over the heads of the crowd. 'You vipers! Who warned you to flee from the wrath to come? You must show yourselves penitent before you come to me for baptism. And don't think you will get a free pass into the Kingdom of Heaven just because you can call yourselves children of Abraham. God can raise up plenty of them out of these stones, if He needs to.'

'Who are you? And why are you here?' they asked him. 'Are you the Messiah?'

'I am not,' John replied flatly.

'Do you call yourself a prophet?'

'No,' he answered.

'Then account for yourself,' they ordered him. 'We have to take word back to the Temple about you.'

John looked directly at them and quoted Isaiah.

'I am the voice of one crying in the wilderness, *Make straight the way of the Lord!*'

'If you are neither the Messiah nor a prophet,' they answered, 'what are you doing here, and why do you baptize?'

'I baptize with water,' John replied, 'but I am no one. You may not know it, but already the one who is greater than I is walking among you. I would go down on my knees to him, but I am not worthy even to undo the strings of his sandals.'

The deputation went back to Jerusalem. The Temple which they represented was the seat of power in Israel, and the ruling body was called the Sanhedrin. On it sat the High Priests – there should have been only one, but the Romans had deposed Annas and put another man, Caiaphas, in his place. Some Jews continued to recognize Annas, however, because the appointment of a High Priest was a matter in which no one who was not a Jew could have any authority. Besides the High Priests, the Sanhedrin was made up of the Chief Priests of the Temple, the Elders, Rabbis (Scribes), members of the families of the past and present High Priests who were called Sadducees, and some Pharisees. As Israel was a theocracy, the highest in the land were the families of High Priests, that is the Sadducees. They were rich and powerful and all lived in or near Jerusalem. The Pharisees were a middle-class sect, and people all over the country belonged to it. There were Pharisees on the council of every Synagogue in the land and they regarded themselves as the special guardians of the Law. It was they who kept watch so strictly over the observance of every tiniest part of it.

There had been both Pharisees and Rabbis in the deputation which went to see John, and he spoke to them as he did because they had become so tyrannical and self-righteous.

After they had gone, John continued where he had left off.

He led the latest comers down to the side of the Jordan and into the water. He pressed them down till the water closed over their heads, and brought them up gasping and spluttering with the fear of being drowned. But that was part of the ceremony, to bring death to their old sins, and new life as they rose up out of the water.

Thousands came to him there from all over Judea, and even from Galilee. Often he shouted at them as he had done when he saw the Temple men coming, for they had to be startled out of their regular habits. One day, in the silence following such an outburst, a man came walking out of the crowd towards him, smiling a little – almost as though at the echo of John's tone.

It was Jesus, come from Galilee to see him and be baptized. There was nothing to suggest to the crowd that he was different from themselves. Even John recognized no more than that here was a man who did not need to be called to repentance. He half shook his head as their eyes met.

'I should come to you,' he said quietly, 'yet you come to me!'

'Let it be so,' Jesus replied, 'it is right that we should start from the beginning in all righteousness.'

The storm had died out of John. His voice had dropped. He walked humbly as he and Jesus went to the river's edge. He lowered Jesus into the water, down on to the river bed. Jesus came up, and stood on the bank with the water streaming off him. It was then that a dove flew down and lighted on his shoulder, and both Jesus and John heard a voice which said: *'This is my beloved Son.'*

John had always believed that he would know when the Great One came. He had expected a sign, and now he recognized it in the dove and the voice.

This was the man for whom the way was to be prepared. John looked at him standing there on the bank, still as though deep in thought, his eyes alive with the impact of

all that had come to him too with those words. No more was
said, and Jesus turned away and was lost in the crowd.
Hardly anyone was aware that anything out of the ordinary
had happened. The crowd was waiting for John to come back
from the river; when he did, coming slowly towards them,
there was a different sound in the familiar words as he said:
'Repent, for the Kingdom of Heaven . . . *is close at hand.*'

Then he added slowly, '*He who was to come after me is
already among you.*'

CHAPTER 6

TEMPTATION

WHEN Jesus turned away and left John and the crowd behind him, he sought some solitary place where he could pray and think undisturbed. As he came up through the waters of the Jordan and breathed the air again, he knew that his own call had come. Every instant of his life up to that moment had been a preparation for what lay ahead, but he needed to be sure of God's will, and time in which to seek the means to carry it out.

He knew what people expected, and that the Priests and Rabbis had no true vision of what the Messiah must do for them. Their minds ran on the single question of freedom from Rome, and he knew that if that was to be the one test by which they would recognize the Messiah and believe in him, then he would certainly be rejected.

They wanted a grand demonstration of power – the power that was force. He had to convince them that the power of the spirit was stronger.

Actually, the Sadducees – and that meant the High Priests themselves – did not believe in the coming of the Messiah. They thought it a myth for the ignorant.

They had made their own terms with Rome, swallowing a good deal of pride and accepting much humiliation in big things as well as small, but keeping their wealth and position so long as they collaborated with the Romans.

A Messiah who came without the power to overthrow Rome in a night could make things exceedingly awkward for the Sadducees, but in their opinion Rome was far too powerful for that ever to happen. Yet, if the Messiah really came, it was to be presumed that he could not fail –

so they invented a paradox, that 'He who is to come, never comes.'

Jesus knew these things, and realized from the first that he would have a stiff fight to change their outlook, make them drop their prejudices and accept the truth. He knew very well the warning that Isaiah had uttered, and which Priests and people alike all learned and had forgotten, that the Messiah would be 'despised and rejected of men, a man of sorrows and acquainted with grief'. But to the members of the Sanhedrin, and to many others in Israel, a man who could come as the Messiah and be despised and rejected by the people could be no Messiah. The true Messiah would have all power in his hands, and must use it, they believed, to overthrow the conqueror, Rome; and in that case, who would despise him?

To be their kind of Messiah in fact, he would have to be shaped to their will, not to God's. But, when Jesus had heard the words, 'This is my beloved Son', it had been as though the world had been put into his hands, and he was left to discover for himself how to keep it spinning on its true course.

So he went up into the most desolate of mountains to turn these things over in his mind before God, and to discover the nature of the Messiah God meant him to be.

Again, words of Isaiah's ran in his mind, that the Messiah should open the eyes of the blind, unstop the ears of the deaf, heal the limbs of the cripples: give relief to prisoners, and teach the poor. First and last he was God's messenger, and what he had to do was to listen and to hear, to let the voice of God speak through him. He was not afraid that Isaiah's words meant that he was doomed to failure. He knew that was not so. The end was not predestined. The people had free will. They could assert it any time they chose. They would assert it if he could find the means to touch them deeply enough. God must win in the end, and it was his task to bring that victory nearer.

Forty days he remained in the mountains, fasting. A great work had been put into his hands but, like the patriarchs, Abraham and Moses, he had to discover for himself how it was to be accomplished. He felt great power within him, and knew also that he was entirely free to choose what he would do. Abraham had set out in great faith from Ur at God's bidding. Moses had felt quite unequal to the task of persuading Pharaoh to let the Hebrews go, until he learned to trust God and to act simply as His servant. It was a long lonely wrestling for Jesus as he searched for the means by which to carry out his great task.

After a time he grew hungry, and his eye fell on the flat oval stones which lay about his feet, reminding him of the little loaves his mother used to bake. It seemed a small matter, with that tremendous sense of power, to turn a few of those stones into the bread they resembled. Telling his friends about it later, he called this 'temptation', being tried and tested. Yet it was no more than an idea presented to his mind and rejected. He was never tempted to use his power in that way. He answered the thought as soon as it was expressed, in the words of Moses, that man does not live by bread alone. Man is body and spirit, and the needs of the spirit are more important than those of the body in the long run.

Jesus had been walking about on a mountain which fell away on the east, in a sheer precipitous drop of something between twelve and fifteen hundred feet to the valley below. Once he paused and looked over it, and the thought presented itself that if he leaped over into mid-air, and God prevented his being smashed to pieces, that would certainly attract attention, especially if it happened where there were crowds of people – if, for instance, he cast himself down from a pinnacle of the Temple. But that would not make anyone believe he was the Messiah. Such an act would be forcing the hand of God, *obliging* God to perform a miracle in order to save His son from destruction. This also Jesus regarded as temptation.

He rejected it in words which were again Moses': 'Thou shalt not tempt the Lord thy God'.

A third temptation came. From that same high ridge of rock, looking out over the world, Jesus thought of the people's dream of a great warrior leading them into battle, conquering the Romans and driving them out of the land, conquering the whole world if need be, till Israel reigned supreme. That too might be done – if it was God's way of achieving His purpose. But Jesus knew it was not God's way. Men do not enter God's Kingdom by force. Force is the devil's way. All have to go in humbly of their own desire.

'Get thee behind me, Satan,' Jesus said. 'Thou shalt worship the Lord thy God, and Him only shalt thou serve.'

These were strange ordeals, but he came through them with the voice of God clear and undimmed, the will of God surging through him, and a great happiness possessed him. He was hungrier than ever, but great strength had come back to his body. He strode down the mountain almost singing, to find John and food.

Before he could see him, Jesus heard John's voice. He was still in the centre of a crowd and his words were ringing on the air. When John took in the radiance which filled him, he fell silent. Out of that silence, he stretched out his arms and cried in his deep voice:

'*Behold the Lamb of God!*' Then, in a different tone, 'This is he of whom I have so often spoken. The Lamb of God who will carry away the sin of the world.'

A lamb was generally thought of in connection with sacrifice, as a victim, but John's tone did not suggest that, though it was tender enough. Nor did it suggest the scape-goat who is burdened with guilt for things it did not do. The Messiah was sometimes called 'the Lamb of God', but the crowd did not think of that either. They were not sure what John meant.

'I did not know him at first,' John said. He had had time to think since he had baptized Jesus. Now he told the crowd:

'I did not know the truth about him until that moment, but now I bear witness before you all.'

CHAPTER 7

THREE DAYS' WALKING,
THREE DAYS' TALKING

JOHN was talking to two young fishermen who had come from Galilee to hear him, when Jesus came towards them. John touched the nearest man on the shoulder and pointed towards Jesus.

'Behold the Lamb of God!' he said, as he had done to the crowd earlier.

The fishermen glanced up and watched the stranger go by. They half started after him, but hesitated until John waved them on. Then, with a laughing farewell, they hurried on. Jesus heard them and turned round.

'What is it?' he asked.

They looked at him, and for a moment forgot to answer, then said 'Where do you live?'

'Come and see,' Jesus replied, and led the way to his lodging. All night they stayed with him, talking.

One of the men became Jesus' closest friend. His name was John. The other was called Andrew, and was so stirred by Jesus' ideas that he ran out first thing next morning to bring his brother to hear them too.

'Simon,' he cried, 'I've found the Messiah!'

They went back together, and Jesus looking at Simon's strong figure and bright brown eyes, said, 'So you're Simon. I shall call you Peter, which means a rock, because one day you will be strong, like a rock.'

Simon, Andrew, and John all lived on the shores of the Sea of Galilee, between Capernaum and Bethsaida, and as Jesus was ready to return to the north, they travelled together. But first there was someone Jesus wanted to find, another man from Galilee, called Philip. Jesus invited him to join them, and in that moment Philip too felt that something immensely important was happening to him.

'I'll come!' he cried eagerly, 'but there's a man I'd like to get hold of first.'

Jesus went back to the others while Philip went to look for a friend whose home was only a few miles from Nazareth, at a village called Cana. Philip was out of breath when he came upon him, and gasped out.

'Nathanael! We've found him! The Messiah! He's Jesus of Nazareth, the son of Joseph the carpenter.'

His friend smiled indulgently. Like many other young men, he had been thinking and talking a great deal lately about the Messiah and the old prophecies. But from Nazareth! None of the prophets so much as mentioned Nazareth. The Messiah was to come out of Bethlehem – and they did not know that Jesus had been born in Bethlehem. Nathanael's eyebrows were raised ironically as he looked into Philip's hot face.

'The Messiah?' he repeated quizzically. 'From Nazareth? Can any good thing come out of Nazareth?'

Philip caught hold of him impatiently.

'Come and see,' he cried. 'Just come, that's all.'

He tugged his sleeve, and Nathanael followed. So they came towards Jesus, who smiled as he remarked: 'Here comes an Israelite in whom there is no guile!' meaning, 'There's no pretence here. He's an honest fellow.'

'Why do you say that?' asked Nathanael.

Jesus surveyed him with an expression rather like the one Nathanael himself had worn when Philip found him.

'I saw you under the fig tree,' he said, 'before Philip reached you.'

They looked at one another. Nathanael wondered how much Jesus knew of what had been in his mind as he had stood thinking in the shade of the fig tree. Could his thoughts have been visible? Under Jesus' steady gaze he felt exposed. Slowly, as though the words were forced out of him, he said:

'You are the Son of God, the King of Israel.'

Jesus' tone was still light as he replied, 'What, all that because I said I saw you under the fig tree? I tell you, you will see things much more surprising before long.'

They set out then for Galilee, 'home' to all of them, by the road over the hills, carrying food for the journey with them. At night they wrapped themselves in their cloaks and lay down to sleep under the stars, for it was March again, and there was spring in the air.

Each of them caught a glimpse during that walk of what Jesus' coming might mean. He talked to them of how the Kingdom of Heaven must come here on earth, though it could not be a kingdom in the political sense, and would not have the kind of king man sets up. A sense of tremendous possibilities stirred in them as Jesus talked about truth, basic everlasting truth, with the suggestion that they would find it in themselves. 'The Kingdom of Heaven is within you,' he said, and 'The truth sets you free.'

They could not see how it worked, but only that if it did, miracles might happen. It felt like tugging and pulling at an unfamiliar knot, too impatient to remember that it was a straight piece of string and the twisting of the thread could be traced if they worked at it.

Three days' walking, three days' talking!

The five men had all been fired by John the Baptist's talk, but now they had to get their bearings all over again, to see how his teaching and the new things Jesus was telling them went together. John spoke continually of repentance, with a tongue that lashed. Suddenly they felt that John was already a voice of the past, but what Jesus promised they thought they recognized as true and everlasting.

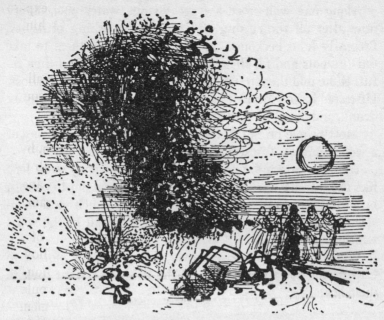

How they talked and argued on that journey! Not only with Jesus but among themselves, now pressing close, now two or three striding ahead to settle a point between them, then turning back to face the others, voices rising and falling, spurts of laughter, shouts of comprehension, shriller cries of disagreement and rejection.

Nathanael had to be home for a wedding, and it turned out that Jesus and his mother were going to it also. The other four could hardly bear to part with Jesus so soon, and he said, 'Come too.'

Mary had gone ahead to help with the preparations. She was anxious when she saw Jesus with extra guests. It would be embarrassing if the wine ran out. 'Don't worry. It will be all right,' Jesus assured her. 'Just wait till the time comes.'

He was sitting near enough for her to whisper to him, and she warned the servants behind her to come if Jesus called them.

Along one wall stood six great stone water pots, empty now after all the rinsing of hands and washing of dishes. Presently Jesus beckoned the servants and told them to take out the pots and fill them again at the well. When they returned he told them to take a cup out and carry it to the host. He tasted it, and found it better than the wine he had already drunk, and he called to the bridegroom:

'Most people bring out their best wine at the beginning of a wedding feast. You seem to have kept yours to the end!'

To turn water into wine at a marriage feast may seem very like the wonder-working Jesus was determined not to permit, but what happened at Cana was not so much a demonstration of power, as the first shining through of the spirit which inspired belief.

When the festivities were over, Jesus took his mother to Capernaum for a few days, and the fishermen went back to their boats.

CHAPTER 8

THE MAN WHO CAME BY NIGHT

THE Passover was only a few days off. Jesus would have gone to Jerusalem for it in any case, but this year not merely to take part in it like any one of the thousands of pilgrims. Now, though he had not declared himself, he went as 'He who should come', a man of mystery, doing astonishing things for reasons that were not obvious. He had two centres on which to work, the country people and the men of the Temple. He chose to start on the latter in Jerusalem at the Passover.

As a boy, he had thought with fervour of the Temple as his Father's house. He returned to it, a man of thirty, knowing quite surely the magnitude of the task that had been laid upon him. There again, in what had been intended to be a 'House of Prayer for all nations', he was met by the uproar of the traders. The ground of Solomon's Porch was slippery with muck, and the air foul with the stench of the beasts. It was only what he expected. It was there he meant to strike his first blow. This unseemly traffic was permitted, actually encouraged, by the Priests and Elders because it was so profitable, and they shut their eyes to the offence it gave to all pious Jews.

Some of his friends had come from Galilee with Jesus and walked with him through the Porch, between the herds of oxen and flocks of sheep, avoiding the great wicker cages where doves fluttered uneasily. They were jostled by porters shouting, 'Make way, make way!' as they took their short cuts through the Temple with their loads.

Then Jesus stooped quietly and picked up some cords which were lying about. John and Simon watched in surprise as he plaited them together, making a whip with a hand-grip, the long ends free. Then he ordered the traders out, and drove them and their cattle towards the gates. He flung over the exchange tables, and sent the piles of coin rolling, but he took care not to frighten the doves. 'Take these things away,' he said to the man in charge of the cages.

The Porch was soon in an uproar, with traders protesting loudly as they tried to control their stampeding flocks. Sheep scattered as they escaped from the pens. Behind them all came Jesus, flicking his whip, driving them before him, out of the House of God crying, 'You turn my Father's house into a den of thieves.'

His friends felt anxious, thinking he had not considered the consequences.

There were Temple guards on duty, and when they saw what was happening, they came to Jesus and asked what it meant, and by what right he had interfered with what was a regular procedure.

These men were accustomed to keeping order, and if necessary they dealt sharply with those who resisted them, but Jesus too had an air of authority which they found themselves respecting. But what he said in reply seemed to them no answer. He said, 'Destroy this Temple, and in three days I will raise it up.' (It became of great importance later to remember the exact words he used.)

The guards looked at him scornfully.

'This Temple has taken forty-six years to build,' they told him, 'forty-six years, and you say you could raise it up in three days!'

But Jesus, for his own reasons, had spoken of himself and not the building. All that the Temple had originally stood for to the Jews, as housing the very presence of God, was already weakened and fading, for its holiness had not been preserved. Jesus himself was soon to mean to the whole world what the

Temple had represented to the Jews through the ages – but hardly anyone could have understood that then.

The officers went back to the Council chamber in the Porch and reported the matter to members of the Sanhedrin. The men of the Temple were displeased but they did not regard what had happened as necessarily serious, and for the remainder of the Feast, Jesus was able to teach in the Temple Courts. He entered into disputation with the learned Rabbis, as he had listened and asked questions as a boy. In Jerusalem he healed some of the sick among the pilgrims, and the things he did attracted attention. People followed him about, only half listening, but excited about the miracles, and hoping to see more of them, but Jesus knew he was not touching their hearts.

Like other pilgrims, Jesus was probably sleeping at night outside the city, perhaps over on the slopes of the Mount of Olives, and one night a man came looking for him after dark, with his face hidden in his cloak which, with its broad coloured border, showed that he was a Pharisee. He was in fact an important member of the Sanhedrin. His name was Nicodemus. He addressed Jesus as 'Rabbi', showing him the respect due to a teacher, and his tone was admiring, yet cautious.

'We believe you must have come from God,' he said. 'No one could do what you have been doing here, if God was not with him.'

He did not explain who he included with himself in that 'we'. He had been struck by what Jesus had been teaching in the Temple, was really stirred by it, but did not want anyone to know that. The secrecy with which he had come showed his fear of what other members of the Sanhedrin would say if they knew of it. Nevertheless Jesus saw that he had faith and tried to fan it into flame. He spoke to him from the heart, as he had done to John and Simon, who were probably with him, and told him at once that the new way of life which led into the Kingdom could not be adopted by stealth.

'I warn you,' he said, 'the new and the old cannot grow together – and you stand now for the old. Men have to be *born again* if they are to know what the Kingdom of Heaven means.'

Nicodemus was very conscious of what he stood for in the eyes of the people, of his authority to enforce the strict letter of the Law, and he replied with a touch of irritation, 'How can a man be born again? Can he, when he is old as I am, go back into his mother's womb?'

'Re-born of water and spirit,' Jesus added, 'What comes out of the womb is flesh. Spirit is quite different.'

You can live according to the demands of the flesh – or the inspiration of the spirit. That was what Jesus was telling Nicodemus. If he really meant to accept the new teaching, he must be prepared to go out openly and humbly, like other people, to John, admitting himself wrong, finding penitence, and being baptized.

Of water and spirit ... 'You know the desert wind,' Jesus began to explain, 'it sweeps across the wilderness. You hear it roar as it goes by. You feel it rushing past your cheeks. But you can't take hold of it. You can't produce it to show someone else. They have to hear it and feel it for themselves. It's like that with the spirit.'

Nicodemus shook his head. 'I don't understand,' he said.

Jesus was surprised. 'You!' he exclaimed, 'who teach the young of Israel what to believe, don't you really recognize in your heart what I have been saying? Anyone who has had experience of God should know that much. If you don't understand the things that are part of this life, how will you believe the vaster truths of the heavenly life?'

That bold conception of the spirit flowing so freely, disturbed Nicodemus. There was no freedom and independence in religion as the Pharisees saw it. Their dearest wish was to see the Law so meticulously perfect that no loophole was left for private judgement.

Nevertheless Jesus went on to show him a little more of what the coming of the Messiah must truly mean, and ended with:

'God does not send His son into the world to condemn it but to save it, for He loves the world.'

CHAPTER 9

THE WOMAN AT THE WELL

JESUS had created a sensation when he cleared the traders out of the Temple. It was a challenge which no Jew could misunderstand, but to the authorities in the Temple, it was a plain warning. Many Jews regarded the presence of those rapacious dealers in the Temple, turning it into a noisy street market, as altogether abominable, desecrating the House of God. But they were afraid to say so because the High Priests themselves supported it, and drew a part of their wealth from it.

Even in Jerusalem, what Jesus taught went for the most part in at one ear and out at the other. It was not preaching the people were after, but excitement. The story of the rout of the traders was told everywhere with many additions. The healing too had been exciting, but interest went no further, and Jesus knew it. He decided therefore to return to Galilee, and to deliver there the news of his great message of hope, while he got together a band of helpers, taught them and prepared them to go out as his representatives, and to carry on his work.

Jesus and his five friends left Jerusalem by the road to Jericho, and turned northwards along the Jordan, following John, to continue what he, as the 'forerunner', had begun. They found him still sounding his call to repentance, still baptizing, and Jesus stopped near by, began to preach, and taught his disciples to baptize. The crowds who had come many miles to hear John, went on to Jesus. This disturbed John's followers who protested.

'Look, Master,' they said, 'that man who came to us down by the Jericho road – the one you witnessed to –

he's baptizing here, and our crowds are going over to him.'

'That's all right,' John told them. 'A man can only give what God has put into him. I always warned you that I was not the Messiah. My task has been to go ahead of him, to prepare for his coming.'

His rugged features and honest brown eyes glowed with such happiness and confidence that the protests died away.

'My light must fade,' he went on, 'you must accept that – and his will increase. I have told you only what any mortal man can of heavenly things. Jesus is different. He speaks of them . . . really as God's mouthpiece.'

The Elders of the Temple were keeping a watchful eye on John, even now that he had moved so far from Jerusalem. The insults he had hurled at the Pharisees and Sadducees could not be forgotten. 'Offspring of vipers!' he had cried when he saw them approaching, and his 'Who warned you to flee from the wrath to come?' had drawn titters from the crowds.

Since the clearing of the Temple, Jesus also had become a suspect in their eyes, and when it was reported that he was with John, drawing even greater crowds, they began to think what they could do to silence both of them. Jesus, realizing their intention, moved on. He had a great deal to do before he returned to argue with the men of the Temple, so he climbed the hills and crossed into Samaria, over which the Sanhedrin had no power. The Samaritans were not true Jews. About 700 B.C., after the Assyrians had carried off thousands of Jews, they brought in nomad tribes who settled in Samaria, married the remaining Jewish peasants, adopted Judaism after a fashion, claiming Jacob as their Patriarch, and built a Temple on Mount Gerizim. When the Jews returned from their long captivity, they denounced these mixed marriages, and enmity grew between them and the Samaritans. Then about 128 B.C. the Jews destroyed the Temple on Mount Gerizim, and great enmity continued between the two peoples.

Normally Jews did not pass through Samaria unless they were in a great hurry, or in parties strong enough to resist attack.

Jesus started early, in the cool of the morning, but it was hot and he was thirsty by the time he reached the heights and stopped by an ancient well, the actual well beside which Jacob had rested many centuries earlier, and it was still called Jacob's Well. It can be seen today, its waters still sweet and cool.

Jesus sat down beside it to rest, while Simon, John, and the others went on to the near-by village of Sychar to buy food. Presently a woman came to fetch water, and as she let down her dipper, Jesus said:

'Give me a drink.'

She glanced sharply at him and said, 'You're a Jew. How can you expect me, a Samaritan and a woman, to do anything for you?'

'I am a Jew,' Jesus replied, 'but more, and if you could see what that meant, *you* would be asking *me* for water, and I should have given it you – *living* water.'

She wondered what that meant. Then remarked, 'The well is deep, and you have nothing to draw water with, so where would you get your living water? Our Patriarch Jacob gave us this well. He actually drank from it, he and his children and his flocks. It was good enough for him. You said *living water* as though it would be better than this. Do you say you're greater than Father Jacob?'

'Those who drink from this well get thirsty again,' Jesus said. 'The water I offer you is from a living *spring* which wells up eternally.'

'Oh, then give me some,' she said half frivolously. 'If I don't get thirsty after it, I shan't have to keep on coming to the well.'

Jesus, looking into her heart, took her by surprise as he said, 'Fetch your husband,' implying that if he gave her the water, she would want to share it with him.

'I have no husband,' she returned quickly.

'True,' Jesus agreed, 'you have had five husbands, but the man you are living with is not your husband.'

'Oh, a *prophet!*' she exclaimed and went on, to cover the half-lie she had told about her husband, 'then perhaps you can tell me which is right, you Jews who worship in Jerusalem, or we Samaritans on Mount Gerizim?'

'Jerusalem or Gerizim – the places won't matter to anyone much longer,' Jesus told her. 'But you Samaritans don't understand what you are worshipping. The Jews do, and the whole world depends on them for salvation. You won't understand that, nor that God is spirit and can only be worshipped in spirit and in truth. Places have nothing to do with it.'

She did not understand him.

'I believe the Messiah will soon come,' she said, and her tone suggested a desire for truth. 'He will explain everything to us.'

Jesus said quietly, answering the feeling behind her words, 'I am he. I who am here talking to you.'

She gave him a quick, searching look, and, without another word, set down her dipper and ran back across the fields to the village. Simon and the others, returning, saw her go. It surprised them that Jesus should have been talking to her, but they passed no remark on it, not even to ask what she wanted. They were beginning to know his ways. They unpacked the food and set it before him, but Jesus refused it, saying that he had had meat they knew nothing of.

John and Simon looked at one another, wondering if the woman had given him food.

'To do the will of Him that sent me and to finish His work, that is meat to me,' Jesus explained.

He had found so many who could not or would not listen, and now this woman who was not a Jew, nor even friendly, had responded in the end to truth as he laid it before her. He looked round at their faces with a half smile.

'You hear people say, Harvest is still four months off – and you know what they mean, what the crops look like, how far the ears have swelled. I tell you – these fields are ripe to harvest. Raise your eyes and see for yourselves.'

They looked, and saw the woman returning with a straggling crowd all running towards them.

She had reached the village breathless, and gasped out her story of a man by the well who might be the Messiah, for he had known all about her as soon as he set eyes on her. He said he was the Messiah. Her friends and neighbours dropped everything and ran back with her in the hope of catching him. They begged him to stay for a while and teach them.

They pleaded for what he was longing to give, and he went with them to the village and remained there for two days teaching and preaching continually. A great many Samaritans accepted him in consequence, and believed in the Gospel.

'Since we have heard for ourselves,' they told the woman who had been by the well, 'we believe that this is truly the Saviour of the world.'

CHAPTER 10

MUCH HEALING

FROM the village by the well, Jesus continued on his way to Galilee with his five companions, but as they approached the hill on which Nazareth stood, they heard that John was in prison. He had denounced Herod the Tetrarch, son of Herod the Great and ruler of Galilee, for his latest 'marriage', which had required two divorces and was illegal and incestuous as the bride was his own niece Herodias and the wife of his half-brother. John had spoken his mind, and Herod had sent soldiers out to arrest him.

That John's important work could be brought to an end like this shocked Simon and the other men deeply, but Jesus seemed hardly surprised. All the same, it made a difference to his plans. The work of his forerunner was over, and had to be undertaken now by Jesus himself, or his helpers. He had to think, and so parted from the others where the road forked. They took the right hand path leading to Capernaum and their homes, while Jesus took the left and went to Nazareth. He climbed the familiar hill alone, passing people who had known him all his life. Some looked up and smiled, others stared, wishing they could hear more of what had happened in Jerusalem.

Jesus went on along the road towards Cana, and presently a man who looked important came hurrying towards him. He was in fact a steward in Herod's Palace. He had heard of the miracles Jesus had done in Jerusalem and came for help. He had a small son, desperately ill, and believed Jesus could cure him if he would. He begged him to go back with him to Capernaum.

'Would you believe without signs and miracles?' Jesus

asked, thinking still of the Nazareth people. 'If you were not in trouble, would you come to me?'

The Steward did not try to answer that. He simply begged Jesus to come at once. '. . . before my boy dies.'

'Go home,' Jesus said. 'He will live.'

The man accepted his words and went home.

His faith and his great love for the boy gained for him this miracle of healing, the first Jesus performed in Galilee.

He could find no words to express his gratitude, but Jesus understood it. Then he was striding home as fast as he could go, and when he was nearly there, he saw some of his servants hurrying out in search of him. For a moment his heart stood still. He could hardly wait for what they had to tell him, but as soon as they saw him, they called out 'He's better!'

'When?' he asked. 'At what time did the change occur?'

They told him about seven on the day before – exactly at the time when Jesus had said he would live.

After the Steward had left him, Jesus walked on along the same road, thinking that Capernaum might be a better centre now for the work he had to do, better than Nazareth. It would be as well to be on the alert for trouble from Herod, and what he had to do must not be interfered with, but Capernaum was near the frontier, and there were always boats along the shore to take a man out of reach quickly.

Capernaum was a considerable fishing port with quays and a packing station from which fish was distributed to Jerusalem and all parts of the country. There were often hundreds of boats out on the waters of the Sea of Galilee. Simon and Andrew had one of their own, and John and James's father had several. There were good roads too, north to Tyre and Sidon, to Caesarea Philippi and Damascus.

Jesus went down to the Lake, and looked over that blue, blue water to Mount Hermon, its snow cap gleaming in the sunshine and adding a sparkle to the air. It was Mount Hermon, rising almost out of the waters of the Lake, that caused the sudden storms which the fishermen dreaded.

All too soon he was being pointed out as the man who had cured sick pilgrims in Jerusalem, and people began to bring him all their ailing and diseased relations, their sick and crippled friends, dragging them along, or carrying them on their shoulders, tipping them down before him like sacks of potatoes. Each one was to Jesus a poor child of God and his own brother, wretched, suffering, neglected, gaunt and wild-eyed, their bones sticking out of their flesh, flies buzzing over their festering sores. Many of them spent their days in the streets, begging, an eyesore and a nuisance, with no hope of ever being anything else. But if they could be cured, there would be another pair of hands to work, feet to run, another back to carry loads.

Jesus knew that by healing them he must seem just the kind of wonder-worker the people delighted in, and that it would probably hinder his real work – but what else could he do? How could he love each one of them as himself, and leave them in such misery?

Patiently and tenderly he went from one to the next, speaking, touching, healing, and as they found themselves whole men and women again, joy burst through them so that they laughed and shouted, 'Thanks be to God!' It was useless for Jesus to beg them to keep quiet about it. They leaped about, displaying their new strength, boasting of what had been done for them. The more people Jesus healed, the more were brought to him. They came in hundreds, in thousands, and one day he was nearly pushed into the Lake by the crowds jostling to get near him. Stepping aside to save himself, he saw that there were two boats drawn up nearby; one was Simon and Andrew's, the other belonged to Zebedee, the father of James and John who were in the water, cleaning the nets. Simon and Andrew were standing up in their boat, and came at once when Jesus hailed them. They took him aboard and pushed out from the land a little, then Jesus stopped them. They turned the boat about so that he faced the shore, and from there he began to talk to the crowd.

When he came to the end of what he had to say, he told Simon to launch out into deep water, and then to let down his nets.

'All right, I will,' Simon replied. 'We caught nothing all last night, but if you say so, we'll try again now.'

The nets were cast, and a great shoal of fish swarmed into them. The catch was so great that the nets began to tear, and they hailed James and John to come and help. It needed all the strength of the four men to haul them in, and they were so heavy that the boat began to sink under them. Suddenly Simon realized that Jesus had guided both them and the shoal, and he fell on his knees, and cried:

'Leave me, Lord! I'm such a sinful man.'

But Jesus said. 'Come with me and catch *men* from now on.'

Not only Simon, but the other three men put down their gear, and went too. They had no idea where it would lead them, but they knew they had reached a turning-point in their lives. Nothing else mattered, and they gladly dropped everything, to go wherever Jesus led them. Philip and Nathanael were at home, near Cana, but they too went to join Jesus.

These four fishermen, Simon and Andrew, James and John, were the first of Jesus' disciples, his students in training. They were strong, sensible men accustomed to boats and to going out fishing at night on waters that were notoriously treacherous. They had never had to use their minds much, but they were intelligent and practical. Now wherever Jesus gathered a crowd and talked to them, these four listened, and after the talk was over, they asked him about the things they had not understood.

Jesus often talked of the spirit, and the disciples found that as difficult as Nicodemus had. They seemed at first to be unlearning all they had grown up with. Such things as the spirit they had always taken for granted. Now they felt a little like children at a new school, who have been taught everything differently at the old one. The things Jesus was teaching had to be applied to every part of their lives. They had to live by them.

Every Sabbath they went to the Synagogue with him – and that at least they had always done. But it too became a new experience. Anyone who wished to, could read a lesson at the Synagogue service, but usually only people of such standing as Rabbis or Pharisees did so, and when they expounded what they had read, they referred everything back to verdicts and rulings of learned scholars without explaining the substance of what they had read. Jesus had no official standing, but

when he stood up to read he always made the meaning clear
and simple, bringing out what lay behind it. Gradually his
disciples began to see the Scriptures differently, and the
new explanations were often quite contrary to what the
Pharisees taught.

On their first Sabbath together at the Capernaum Synagogue, Jesus read a passage and returned the Scroll to the
Superintendent, but before he could say anything more, a
man shouted:

'Let us alone, you Jesus of Nazareth! We have nothing to
do with you. Do you want to destroy us! Oh, we know who
you are! The Holy One of Israel!'

The congregation was shocked, as much by what he had
said, as by his having one of his fits during service. Then,
they heard Jesus say, 'Be quiet and come out of him.'

The man flung himself about violently, his whole body
twisted and wrenched in frightful convulsions, in the middle
of which he gave a loud shriek and was suddenly calm and
sane again.

'What happened?' People glanced stealthily at one
another.

'The demon seemed to obey him,' they thought.

When the service was over and they all streamed out into
the sunshine, they looked for Jesus, but he and his companions had slipped away to Simon's house.

Simon's mother-in-law had gone to bed with a touch of
fever and nothing had been prepared. Jesus went in, took her
hand and drew her gently to her feet. At his touch the fever
left her, and she got up and went about her work.

He stayed there for the rest of that afternoon. The Sabbath
Laws kept everyone at home, for no one was allowed to travel
more than two thousand cubits – about five-eighths of a mile
– and that was generally used up going to the Synagogue and
home again. But the Sabbath ended at sundown and its re-

strictions were lifted. Then there was a rush to bring all the chronic and incurable cases to Jesus until it seemed as though the whole city was gathered round Simon's mother-in-law's door.

Hour after hour Jesus healed and ministered to them, all through the evening and on to the small hours of the morning. Then very tired, he went out alone up into the hills to find rest and refreshment.

Before many hours had passed, the house was surrounded again, and Simon and his brother went to find Jesus, but he would not return. Good though it was to heal, that was not his main task. He did not want people to follow him just for benefits of that kind, but to listen to the message he had to give them. So he said, 'No, we must go on.'

CHAPTER 11

NOT DEAD, BUT SLEEPING

O NE day, as they were walking through a place where lepers lived among the caves, one ran out, and flung himself on the ground in front of Jesus, crying desperately: 'If you would, you could heal me!'

Looking down at the white leprous skin and terrible sores, Jesus had compassion on him. The healing power flowed through him, and he said. 'I will. Be clean. Show yourself to the priest, and make the proper thankoffering – and don't talk about it!'

One day when Jesus was teaching, and had a great crowd about him, he noticed a man elbowing his way through as though he had an urgent message to deliver. He was Jairus, the superintendent of the local Synagogue. As soon as he reached Jesus, he threw himself on his knees and cried:

'O Sir, my little daughter is dying. I beg you, to come and make her better.'

Jesus did not say to him, as he had done to Herod's steward, *Go home, she will live,* but promised to go with him, and as he turned about, the crowd streamed after him, so that he could hardly set one foot in front of the other. Among them was a woman who for years had suffered from a chronic bleeding. She had been rich, but had spent all her money going from doctor to doctor, and none of them had done her any good. She had heard what wonderful powers Jesus had, and thought that if she could only touch him – or even just his cloak – she would be well, and he need never know. But as she laid her hand lightly on him, Jesus stood still and asked, 'Who touched me.'

Simon cried out, 'Master, look how they're all pushing to get near you! How can you ask who touched you?'

'I felt the power go out,' Jesus replied.

The instant she touched his cloak, the woman knew that she was healed, the bleeding had stopped. Now, though half afraid, she went down on her knees and admitted what she had done.

'That's all right,' Jesus told her quietly. 'Go in peace. Your faith has brought you this relief. You will have no more of your trouble.'

Meanwhile, someone else from Jairus's home had been struggling through the throng and called out:

'It's no use. She's dead. Don't bother the Master.'

'Steady,' Jesus said to Jairus instantly. 'Don't get frightened, just believe.' He told the crowd to go home, beckoned Simon, James, and John to him, and they went on together. As the sound of mourning reached them Jesus asked, 'Why do you make all this noise? The child is not dead, but sleeping.'

'Not dead?' they retorted. 'Of course she's dead,' and they raised their voices again, for they were hired to wail.

Jesus sent them away, and went in to the child with her father and mother. She was twelve years old; he bent over her, took one of her small hands in his, and said:

'*Talitha cumi!* I'm calling you. Wake up, child!'

The parents could hardly believe it as she opened her eyes

'*Talitha cumi!* Wake up, child!'

and sat up. She got to her feet and walked across to them. Jesus said to her mother, 'Get her something to eat,' and to Jairus, 'Keep it to yourselves. Don't talk about it outside.'

About this time he went back to Nazareth for a visit, and as usual went to the Synagogue on the Sabbath. There, among the people he had known all his life, he stood up to read a Lesson. He was handed the book of Isaiah, and read:

'The spirit of the Lord is upon me, He hath anointed me to preach the gospel to the poor, to heal the broken-hearted, to release captives, to give sight to the blind, and liberty to the oppressed. To proclaim the acceptable year of the Lord.'

He rolled it up again, and gave it back. The eyes of everyone were upon him as he sat down to talk about what he had just read.

They listened, astonished at his wisdom, and his air of authority, though they did not much like it.

'How can he talk like that?' they muttered. 'He's only the carpenter's son, isn't he? We've known him all his life, him and his family.'

'This day these words are actually fulfilled,' Jesus ended.

That shocked them. He was claiming to be the Messiah! Their resentment turned to furious rage. This was presumption – more, it was blasphemy. They got up and drove him out of the Synagogue. He was surrounded by angry men forcing him through the streets and up to a point where the ground fell away precipitously. They were taking the law into their own hands, intending to throw him over to certain death.

But that was not in their power. God's work was not yet done, and Jesus passed between them unnoticed and went away, leaving them struggling with each other, thinking each back turned must be his, getting angrier as they found it was not. And Jesus went on his way, back to Capernaum.

CHAPTER 12

THE MEANING
OF RIGHTEOUSNESS

JESUS continued to heal and to preach. His healing power was so amazing that he was talked about everywhere, and sick people were carried to him from as far as twenty or thirty miles away. He sometimes healed for days on end, with hardly a break for rest or food. Healers today know what it takes out of them, and Jesus also found it exhausting. There came a day when he had to rest, and he sent Simon and John to bring round a boat so that he could escape for a while. They rowed out in the late afternoon across the Lake, and Jesus drew his cloak about him and fell asleep.

It was growing dark when they put in to a deserted beach, and Jesus went away alone into the hills, to spend the night in prayer and that communion with God which was greater refreshment to him even than sleep.

He came out to Simon and John next morning, walking from between a fold of the hills, and saw a crowd again waiting for him lower down. There was by this time always an inner circle of men and women who were part of every crowd, but always in the front, eager to learn, ready to talk and ask questions. The others rarely spoke, except to exclaim as they watched the miracles. For them Jesus had nothing that day though he did not send them away.

He sat down on a rock and began to call his men to him, Simon and John, always first in his plans, then their brothers, Andrew and James, then Philip and Nathanael, and Levi who had been the tax collector. His eyes roved over the rest of that inner circle, who were all looking eagerly towards him. He

78

called five more, Thomas, another James, another Simon, Thaddeus, and finally Judas Iscariot, the only one among them who did not belong to Galilee.

These twelve were to be his representatives, his 'apostles', and Jesus began to prepare them for their great task, to show them as simply as possible what it meant to become part of the Kingdom of Heaven. It was their special instruction, and what we know of it is what these twelve men remembered for the rest of their lives and handed on. Most of them were dead

when it came to be written down. It is to be found in the fifth, sixth, and seventh chapters of the Gospel of St Matthew, and is called 'the sermon on the Mount'. It is still regarded as the great code of human behaviour for all Christian people.

It declares that, before all else, we have to choose righteousness, that we are free, and can choose to please ourselves. We can take the way of the world if we like, and enjoy our fun, ignoring that we are spirit as well as flesh.

But choose righteousness, Jesus told them, as hungrily as you choose good food for your body. *They that hunger and thirst after righteousness will be filled.*

Don't mind not being important or being poor. Strive for the true humility of saints and very great men. *Blessed are the meek, for they shall inherit the earth.*

Give to all, share all you possess. Be merciful. *Blessed are the merciful. To them mercy will be shown.*

When you mourn for someone you loved, their death brings you nearer God, and you learn as you are comforted. *Blessed are they that mourn, for they shall be comforted.*

Keep your hearts as pleasant places where God can come and rest. *The pure in heart are blessed, for they shall see God.*

Be peacemakers, for they are indeed God's children.

He went on, 'You now become the light of the world, and must hand on that light. Light is not easily hidden. A city built on a hill catches the eye and there is no way of hiding it. Your light is kindled by God. Take care that it shines out so that all men see it.

'You must take care that your righteousness goes deeper than that of the Scribes and Pharisees,' Jesus went on. 'Study the words of the Law for yourselves, and see what it means. The sixth commandment is *Thou shalt not kill*: why do men kill? Isn't it out of hatred, out of passionate, unreasoning anger? Clear up every grievance as you go along, don't let them run on and take hold of you. Whenever you go up to the altar with a gift, think first whether anyone has cause to feel wronged by you. If so, leave your gift, find that man and make it up with him. When you return, your offering will be acceptable to God.

'The third commandment forbids you to swear falsely, but I say, Swear not at all. Let your word be a plain Yes, or No.

'You have been taught, "an eye for an eye and a tooth for a tooth" – but I say never return evil for evil. Don't hit back. Accept the blow.

'Give when you are asked to, help those who want to borrow. These things are all *loving your neighbour* – but you are more accustomed to hear, *Love your neighbour and hate your enemy*. I say love your enemy. When anyone abuses you, or ill-treats you, go to God, and pray. So you will become

God's children, and remember He keeps the sun rising over good and bad alike. He sends the rain on both sides of the fence, both to you and to your enemy.

'What is the use of loving only the people who love you? Your task is to be perfect, as your Father in Heaven is perfect.

'When you make a gift, don't have trumpets blowing, as some people do in the Synagogue, to draw attention to the size of their gift. Give so secretly that even your left hand does not know what your right is doing.

'When you fast, look cheerful. Show a fresh face to the world, brush your hair as carefully as usual, and let no one guess that you are denying yourself.

'And now about prayer: When you pray, don't stand about in the streets, praying aloud for other people to hear and admire you. Go into your room and shut the door. The thing done in public brings its own reward when people say – "How good he must be!" – The Father sees what is done in secret, and that is all that matters.

'Don't rattle off a lot of empty phrases over and over again as though the number of times you say them, or the time you spend over them, are likely to please God specially.

'And remember when you pray, that the Father knows what you need before you ask for it.'

Then he gave them the prayer which is used still all over the world, in all languages, by every kind of person.

'When you pray,' Jesus said to the twelve apostles, 'say –

Our Father which art in heaven, Hallowed be Thy Name.
Thy kingdom come.
Thy will be done, on earth as it is in heaven.
Give us this day our daily bread.
And forgive us our debts as we forgive our debtors.
Lead us not into temptation, but deliver us from evil.'

He went on to speak about *Treasure* – the things people set their hearts on.

'Don't load yourselves with possessions,' he said. 'Thieves break in to steal what they too regard as treasure. Moths get in and ruin fabric and furs. Rust eats into metal. Then what is your treasure worth? Whatever it is, you will have given your heart to it – so lay up for yourselves treasure that thieves cannot steal, nor moth nor rust destroy. Choose treasure in heaven. No one can serve two masters. You will always prefer one or the other, and you have all to choose in the end between God and your possessions.

'But there is no need to fret about material things, about what to eat, what to wear, how you will manage as the years go by. God knows what you need. The body is more important than the clothes you dress it in, and life far more than the food to keep you alive. Can you make yourself grow by worrying about your size? As to clothes – think of the wild flowers. They neither sew nor spin, yet Solomon in all his glory was not so wonderfully arrayed – and they live only from today till tomorrow, and are withered. Do you think God who made them so beautiful will fail to clothe you also, O ye of little faith? But before everything else, you must choose righteousness and seek the Kingdom of God. After that, you will find all you need put into your hands. Take each day as it comes, and don't fret about the next. Sufficient unto the day is the evil thereof.'

The sermon was nearly over, so was the day. What Jesus had been delivering to them was – his message, the very Word of God. The crowd heard him in stillness and silence.

'Judge not, and you will not be judged,' Jesus began again.

'How is it,' he asked, 'that you notice other people's faults so much more easily than your own? You rush to set one another right, but can't see that you yourselves are wrong. Look at yourself first, then when you are perfect see what you can do for the others. Love your neighbour, do to others only what you would like them to do to you. That is the Law, and right by the prophets too.

'You do not like it when people take your things: then do not take other people's things. You don't like it when people tell stories about you which are not quite true, so don't make up stories about others.'

Again Jesus told them to ask, to seek, and to knock, for everyone that asks, receives; those who seek, find; to those who knock, the door will be opened.' He told them always to believe in the loving kindness of God. 'Is there anyone here who would pick up a stone and give it to a child who was asking for bread? And you are only human. Your Father in Heaven is always far more loving.

'Everyone is known by the things he does and says, just as you recognize a tree by its fruit,' Jesus went on, 'Fruit growers know the apple trees in their orchards and can tell pretty well what sort of a crop each should produce. If any go on year after year not yielding, they are cut down, so see that you bear good fruit and a good crop every year.

'You know it is not enough to put on a suitable look, and say *Lord, Lord!* You have to try to do right. You have to choose to do right.'

Those who choose righteousness are like good pioneers setting out across unknown country. They make sure of the ground before they begin to build. They can build safely on rock, but sand would shift under the foundations, so that when storms came the whole house might collapse.

'You who listen to me and take heed of what I say will be like the wise man who built his house on rock. Winds may batter you, rains beat down, flood surge round your walls – but your house will stand firm.'

'He gives me new faith,' said a listener.

But to the twelve chosen men who had the beginnings of understanding, it was a strange and difficult lesson, unlike anything heard before from the mouth of any Rabbi.

CHAPTER 13

WHAT WENT YOU OUT FOR TO SEE?

BIGGER and bigger crowds came day after day to Jesus, pressing about him to listen, hoping vaguely for something – they did not quite know what – and Jesus felt great pity for them.

'Sheep, without a shepherd,' he said to his disciples, 'but you can see that the harvest is promising. If only we had men enough to gather it in! Pray all of you, that the Lord will send us labourers so that all may be safely brought into His barns.'

He had chosen these twelve as the first of the labourers, and now they were ready to be sent out. He drew them round him for their final instructions. and told them to work in pairs and to go, on this occasion, only to Jews, to 'the lost sheep of Israel'. Later he would send to the Samaritans and other Gentiles. They were to proclaim everywhere the fact that the Kingdom was close at hand, but they were not to try to teach. Their task was to heal and to make the coming of the Kingdom known. They would find they had the power to cure all kinds of sickness, even lepers and madmen.

They were to take no thought for what they would eat or what they would wear, but to trust God to provide all that was needful. They were to carry no food in their packs, no drink in their flasks, no change of shoes or garments.

'When you come to a town or village,' Jesus told them, 'find a place to stay and ask the people there if they will have you. Greet them with a blessing and say, "Peace to this house!" Stay there till your work is done if they welcome you. If you are turned away, take back your peace and go.'

He warned them to be prepared for difficulties.

'I am sending you out like sheep going among wolves,' he said. 'Be wise as serpents and gentle as doves! But even so you may run into trouble. You may be brought before the Elders in the Synagogues, even before the Council. You may be flogged. What they hate in me, they will hate in you. Whatever happens, don't get frightened. Have no anxiety about how to defend yourselves. The right words will come, and it will not be you speaking, but God through you.'

He repeated that they should not stay where they were unwelcome.

'You must not be upset about all this,' he said comfortingly. 'There is no need to fear men what at worst can only destroy the body and kill you. They can't hurt your spirit. Only God can destroy body *and soul*.'

On the face of it there was not much comfort in that, yet it did make sense. Those who have refused to choose righteousness and go their own way to the end of their lives, may die without having done any of the things they were born for. Then they are not the people they were meant to be – and that by their own choice. If they persist right to their deathbeds, they die with nothing left but a worn-out body and a spirit that has never functioned. The furnace burns them up completely.

'The very hairs of your head are known to the Father,' Jesus told them, 'and remember, not a sparrow falls to the ground without His knowledge and concern, and you are more precious to Him than many sparrows.'

The Apostles had not long been gone when two men came in search of Jesus. They were from John the Baptist who was still languishing in Herod's dungeon with hope fast fading, and doubts creeping insidiously into his mind. There beside the Jordan he had been so sure that he recognized Jesus as the Messiah, the Christ. Now he was troubled about it. Where were the mighty deeds he had expected, the overthrow of the

strong, the raising up of the weak? No mountains had been levelled to the ground, no valleys filled. He had listened in vain for the sound of the woodsman's axe crashing through the trees. He even half expected his own prison walls to fall, the door of his cell to fly open – for Isaiah had spoken of the release which the Messiah would bring to captives, and he was a captive, bound, and unjustly.

Doubts tortured him in the loneliness of his prison, and his faith failed. He got a message to his disciples and begged them to go to Jesus and ask him plainly, 'Are you he who is to come, or do we wait for another?'

That question Jesus heard with a chill of disappointment. John, of all people, to have lost faith!

'Go back and tell him to reconsider what he knows,' he told the messengers. 'Tell him that the blind see, the lame walk, the deaf hear. Lepers are cleansed, even the dead have come back to life. And the people hear the news of the coming of the Kingdom.'

There was a pregnant silence before he added slowly, 'But blessed is the man who does not lose faith in me.'

The men went away, and Jesus, standing before a waiting crowd, looked over the sea of faces and wondered who could be expected to grasp this new thing of the Kingdom if not John – John, who had been appointed through the ages as the forerunner, John who had in fact prepared the way for him.

John had preached, *Repent, for the Kingdom of Heaven is at hand.* He had recognized Jesus and acclaimed him. He had sent him the most eager of all his followers. Now all the might, all the power, he had looked for had arrived – but to work through love, not force: by reason and persuasion, not violence. Had he missed it in the end?

Suddenly Jesus' voice rang out, and he was greatly moved.

'What did you expect to see when you all trooped out to the desert after John? A wild man shouting about something he did not understand? A mere reed shaken by the wind? What did you go out to find? Were you expecting a Prince, or a High Priest? No! They don't make their homes in caves. They don't wear hair-shirts! Then what were you after?'

No sound answered him.

'He was a Prophet!' Jesus cried. 'That was what you expected and that was what you found. But he was more than a Prophet! He was the man singled out through all the history of our people to prepare the way for the coming of the Son of man. Oh, I tell you, no greater man than John was ever born of woman.'

Grief echoed through his words, for he loved John. He added:

'Yet the humblest member of the Kingdom of Heaven is greater than he.'

There was another silence which held the people still and silent.

'It is little more than a year since he began preaching

beside the Jordan,' Jesus went on. 'Between then and now what eager crowds came to him to discover the way into the Kingdom! Can you understand when I tell you that the whole of the Law and all the wisdom of the Prophets were in preparation for this – and now John doubts it. John, who (if you can believe it) is the very Elijah of the Prophets! O you who have ears to hear, hearken to my words!

'Since John came baptizing,' Jesus began again, 'I tell you the gates of the Kingdom of Heaven have been thrown wide open, and eager souls have been rushing in to take it by storm. The people who went to John and were baptized – and there were many publicans and sinners among them – *were fulfilling the purposes of God*, carrying out the plan He made for the world. The Scribes and Pharisees who set themselves against John and would have no part in his baptism, were opposing the will of God. With the doors wide open, they would not go near them if they had to enter through him, and he was God's messenger.

'Oh, how can I make you understand? You are like bands of children in the market-place, each playing their own games and refusing to join in and play together. One party complains, "We played at weddings and you wouldn't dance!" and another, "*We* played at funerals, and *you* wouldn't wail!"

'John expected disasters – I want you to rejoice – because the Kingdom of Heaven is near. But you won't accept either. John lived like a hermit, wore a hair shirt, fasted, and half starved himself. I came among you eating and drinking like anyone else – and you complain of us both. You say he's mad, and the other is a glutton, too fond of the good things of this world.'

As though God had heard his anguish and had answered him, Jesus suddenly raised his head and gave Him thanks. Indeed, a new understanding did then come to him, with the assurance that God had put everything into his hands, the task and the power to do it, though the means he had still to find.

'Come unto me all ye that labour and are heavy laden,' he said to the crowd. 'Take my yoke on your shoulders. It is easy and my burden is light.'

CHAPTER 14

LOAVES AND FISHES

JOHN'S end was near. Herodias had never forgiven his denunciation of her 'marriage' to Herod, her uncle. She had urged Herod to put him to death, but the Tetrarch was weak, obstinate, and superstitious. Several times he had had John brought up from his dungeon to talk to him, and had been surprised at his wisdom and good sense. He had even adopted some of John's ideas. But John's attitude to the 'marriage' did not change, and could not. Yet Herod did not relish the idea of killing a prophet. It was sure to bring him trouble. The people believed in John, and might rebel if he were killed. Herod only kept his crown so long as he pleased the Romans, and rebellion never pleased Rome. So John remained in prison.

At the end of March Herod had a birthday, and ordered a banquet in the Roman style to celebrate it, with dancing girls, also in the Roman style. There Herodias saw her opportunity. Her daughter, Salome, by an earlier marriage, should be one of the dancers. It was unseemly for a Princess of the royal blood, a granddaughter of Herod the Great, to dance in public, and with dancing girls, but Herodias brushed that aside. She should dance first, and alone, specially for Herod.

Accordingly she danced, and Herod mellow with wine and rich food, made much of her, and wondered what gift would be good enough for her. Pearls? Rubies?

'Choose!' he cried. 'Anything you like – to half my kingdom. I take my oath on it!'

Salome ran to consult her mother.

'What shall I have?' she asked breathlessly.

'The head of John the Baptist, on one of the gold platters,' her mother replied – and Salome danced back to Herod.

He was shocked. Jewels he had thought of, even a palace – but this! And he had sworn it before his guests.

Nevertheless he beckoned to a servant and ordered the execution forthwith; and John's head to be brought to the banqueting hall on a platter like another dish for the table.

When John's disciples heard what had happened they went to the prison, took away the body and buried it.

The news came quickly to Jesus, and the Apostles heard it still earlier. They suddenly realized they were actually on Herod's territory, preaching in John's words about the coming of the Kingdom. They were grieved and shocked, but also frightened, in panic they turned and fled back to Jesus.

He saw how tired and troubled they were, and said, 'Come, let us go away by ourselves to a quiet place and talk about this.'

They took a boat across the Lake as they had so often done before, and went ashore near Bethsaida and up towards the hills. But their departure had been seen by people in Capernaum, who stood on the shore to see where the boat was making for, and after it came in, watched the little group against the green of the grass. Then they went round the coast after him.

But that was a day unlike all others, and Jesus' first thought was for his troubled men. John's doubts had distressed him, but to the Twelve the news of his death came as a threat even to their own lives.

Jesus listened and comforted them, and a plan grew in his mind for another great instruction. As evening fell, they saw the crowds that had gathered lower down, and were huddled against the hillside like a flock of sheep. Looking at them, Jesus put a testing question to Philip.

'Look down there,' he said. 'What shall we do about these people? They must be very hungry.'

The disciples never had much money, what they had was in a common purse in Judas's keeping.

Philip replied practically, 'If we had many pounds' worth of bread we could not feed them all.'

Another of the Twelve said impatiently, 'We can't do anything about it. Let us send them away, and they can find food for themselves on their way home.'

'There's a boy here who has a little food with him,' Andrew put in diffidently. 'Five little barley loaves and a couple of small fishes – but what's that among so many?'

'Bring him here,' Jesus said, 'and make all these people sit down in groups, tidily, leaving room for you to pass between them and reach each one.'

No one knew what Jesus was going to do.

He took the boy's little barley loaves and gave thanks for them in the way he always did for food and drink. Then the Apostles carried the bread to the company sitting on the grass, and dropped crumbs into their hands. He did the same with the fish. There was faith there that day. The eyes of everyone were on Jesus. They ate and were fed.

'Gather up any crumbs that remain,' Jesus said when they had finished, 'let nothing be wasted.' And the Twelve brought back to him twelve basketsful.

It was the sort of miracle that roused the crowd all too easily. A *prophet*! they thought, and their hearts glowed. They remembered the prophets of old, and a fever of excitement ran through them. A Prophet? A King? A warrior prince to drive out the legions of Rome?

Jesus saw what was happening, and sent the Apostles away. He wished to be alone with the crowd who were already too excited to hear him speak. Through the babel of voices the cry *Hail, King of the Jews!* was raised and began to echo on all sides. They made a sudden surge towards him, to lift him on to their shoulders and carry him away. But Jesus put them away from him.

When they found that he was actually refusing the honour, they lost their heads and tried to overpower him. But the Son of God was not to be taken by force at the will of a mob. Jesus' Kingdom – the Kingdom of Heaven – was not of the kind to be entered or taken by storm. His task was not to set them free from Rome, but free in spirit.

Quietly Jesus extricated himself, and passed from among them, leaving them wrestling with each other, snatching at arms and garments, pulling men round to see their faces, searching blindly and angrily. And all the time, Jesus was at no great distance from them, in the hills, praying for help and guidance.

When they left him, the Apostles had taken a boat and rowed out a little way so that they could look back at what was happening, but with so much dust in the air, they could not make out if Jesus was there or not. Daylight faded and night came down, and still Jesus did not appear. In the early hours of the morning a head wind from the slopes of snowy Mount Hermon swept over the lake, raising the waves, and the Apostles had hard work to keep their craft steady. It was when the storm was at its worst, in the darkest hour of the night, the hour before dawn, that the near-full moon of the Passover season showed them a white figure by the Lake. It looked ethereal and strange, standing there by the water with the moonlight flooding over it, and the Apostles thought it must be a ghost, but Jesus sang out to them, 'Hallo! It's I. Don't be afraid.'

'Oh, if it's you, Lord,' cried Peter, 'call me to you over the water.'

'Come then,' said Jesus, and Peter scrambled over the side of the boat and stood for a moment, full of faith and confidence, on the surface of the water. Then a gust of wind caught him and he lost his balance. He became afraid, and began to sink. But even as he cried out, 'Save me! Save me!'

Jesus was beside him, caught his arm, and drew him ashore.

'So little faith!' Jesus rallied him lightly. 'What made you doubt?'

The others came in then, filled with awe, and as they stood round Jesus in the dawn, one of them said, 'It is true. You are the son of God.'

Yet the phrase did not really mean the Messiah to them, but simply expressed their awe and wonder.

CHAPTER 15

I AM THEIR BREAD

MANY of those who had eaten that meal had wanted to make Jesus King, and stayed in the hills all night expecting him to come back. When dawn came, and there was no sign of him, they went down to the shore to count the boats which had brought him and to calculate whether the disciples were still about. Some boats had evidently gone, so the men began to drag others down to the water, and set off in them for Capernaum to look for Jesus there.

They found him, and demanded quite angrily how he had got away, asking as though they had a right to know because they had wanted to make him their king.

'You did not see what was being shown you,' Jesus said. 'All you saw was bread, everyday bread. You work for bread. You give all your minds to the needs of the body – but the needs of the spirit you don't even recognize.'

'And what may they be?' they inquired.

'Simply to believe in the food that comes from heaven,' Jesus told them.

He was on his way to the Synagogue where people were waiting for him. When he reached it he went on talking about this heavenly bread, and the men who were feeling so discontented with him, said:

'Moses gave our fathers bread of heaven when they were in the desert, as a sign that God was with them.'

'Not Moses,' Jesus corrected them, 'but God. God gave them the bread, the *manna*, and now He sends you another sort of bread from heaven which is to give you life everlasting.'

I Am Their Bread

As the woman at the well in Samaria had said of the 'living water' after which no one would thirst again, *'Give me that water'* – so these people said, 'Give us that bread, now and for the rest of our lives.' Then they would no longer have to struggle and slave to feed themselves and their families.

'I am the new bread of heaven,' Jesus said, 'like the *manna*, sent you by the Father. Whoever comes to me shall never hunger.'

That was too much for them, and they began to mutter among themselves.

'What does he mean, about being bread of heaven sent by the Father? Don't we all know who and what he is? Isn't he Jesus, the Nazareth carpenter whose mother and father we all know?'

Jesus stopped them quietly.

'When anyone comes to me, it is because he has heard the voice of God within him – and not otherwise. The voice of God is there in your hearts if you will listen. All who listen to it, will come to me.' He went on, 'Yes, your ancestors ate *manna*, and when their time came they all died. The heavenly bread of which I am speaking, will bring you into the Kingdom of Heaven which is life everlasting. *And I am that bread*. I offer you myself, even my flesh and blood; and those who hunger and thirst after righteousness *will find righteousness*, if they will be fed by my flesh and my blood.'

There were, as always, Pharisees and Rabbis among the audience, and what Jesus had just said sent them to their feet in angry protest. Blood of any kind, even in the meat they ate, was abhorrent to Jews. It was one of their oldest laws. The bare mention of it outraged and disgusted them.

'Nevertheless,' Jesus said, knowing well how they felt, 'unless you do this, the spirit will not thrive in you.'

A great many people besides Pharisees and Rabbis took offence at this point, went away, and would not listen to Jesus any more.

'That was too much altogether!' they stormed as they went home.

Jesus watched the Synagogue empty, then he looked at his chosen Twelve, and asked, 'Do you want to go too?'

'To whom could we go now?' Simon Peter asked him with a straight look out of his dark eyes. 'John is dead. The way of eternal life lies in you, Lord, and we believe that you are the Christ, the Son of the living God.'

Still Jesus looked round at them, one after another.

'I chose each of you to be my Apostle,' he said at last. 'Yet – one of you is against me. One of you is working for the devil.'

Eleven of those present did not know what he meant. But Judas Iscariot knew.

When he had seen Jesus actually refuse the leadership of the crowd after the feeding of the five thousand, he had come to a decision, and that was to pursue his own ambition and not God's will. He, like most other people, wanted that worldly Messiah who would conquer Rome. This idea of a spiritual Messiah which Jesus was promising might be all right, but Judas did not believe in it. He was seething inside with anger and disappointment though he showed no sign of it on the surface. Even after Jesus had spoken of the one who was against him, Judas gave no sign. He intended to go on with his own plans yet to remain with Jesus so that he would know all that went on within the inner circle.

That treachery Jesus had recognized.

CHAPTER 16

TO KILL OR TO HEAL?

THE Passover had come round again, and Jesus went up to Jerusalem. He approached the city from the north-east, and came to it past the Pool of Bethesda where the traders used to wash the animals they were bringing to the Temple for sacrifice. The gate nearby was therefore called the Sheep Gate. But the Pool was famous for another reason. From time to time there was a bubbling up in its waters, and the first person to get into it after each disturbance started was cured of his ailments. Five stone shelters had been built round it, and there people waited for the healing moment. Jesus noticed a number of them huddled together as he went by that day, and one in particular who was helplessly crippled. He had been so for thirty-eight years.

'Do you want to be healed?' Jesus asked him.

'Oh yes,' the man cried, 'but I have no one to put me into the water, and while I'm trying to reach it someone else always gets in front of me and I have to wait till the next time.'

'Get up then,' Jesus said. 'Pick up your mat and walk.'

The cripple scrambled up, stood for a moment feeling his feet under him, and then stooped for the mat. He could stand. He could walk. But when he turned to thank Jesus, he was no longer there. He had gone on through the Sheep Gate. This happened on a Sabbath, however, and the man had not gone far carrying his mat before he was stopped by some Elders from the Temple. They spoke sharply to him about breaking the Sabbath.

'The man who cured me told me to,' he explained.

The Elders were at once suspicious.

'What do you mean?' they asked. 'Who has cured you? Who told you to carry your mat on the Sabbath?'

The man did not know who Jesus was, and could not see him anywhere about, so the Elders let him go. Later on Jesus saw him in the Temple and spoke to him.

'Well, so you are cured,' he said. 'See you sin no more lest anything worse happen to you.'

The man was not sure what he meant, but he smiled happily and went to the Elders and told them about it. It was just what they had expected. No one but Jesus dared to defy them and the Law in this way. He seemed always to be breaking the Sabbath and encouraging other people to do so too.

'There's nothing for it,' they told one another angrily. 'We must have that man put out of the way, even if we have to kill him.'

They found him teaching in one of the Courts, and interrupted him to reprimand him for breaking the Law.

It is the fourth commandment which says *Remember to keep holy the Sabbath*, and it goes on to explain that after six days of labour, '*the Lord rested on the seventh day and hallowed it*'. To the Elders these things were quite familiar and it was their duty to understand them. So to them Jesus replied, that God was still working, and therefore he himself worked, even on the Sabbath.

In their eyes that statement made matters far, far worse, for it was blasphemy, putting himself on a level with God.

'You should believe what I say, for it is so,' Jesus warned them. 'I do nothing through any power of my own, but only as God works through me. The Father, loving His son, has shown him all that He does. He raises up the dead, and the son may also bring back to life whom he will. If you will listen, and believe me, you will not enter damnation when you die, but pass from death to life. But again I tell you, I do nothing of myself. I do not seek my own way, but the will of the Father who has put judgement of men in to the hands of

His son, who is also *man*. If you do not honour the son, you
do not honour the Father either.'

Jesus said these things plainly in words the Elders should
have understood. They are difficult for us today, but were in
language familiar to the Jews. But the Elders were saying,
'Does he really think we shall take his word for such
things!'

As though he was answering them, Jesus went on:

'If I were alone in telling you these things, you might fall
back on the law which says there must be two witnesses for
truth to be shown, but you had another witness – John. You
recognized that John was here for a purpose. You sent to him
to find out what that purpose was. He told you the truth
about himself and about me. I need no man's testimony, but I
tell you these things to warn you to save yourselves. John
was a great light shining out of the darkness. For a time even
you welcomed his light. But I have a greater witness even
than John – and that is the work itself which the Father sent
me to do. The very things you object to should show you that
the Father has sent me – the healing, that the blind see, the
deaf hear, cripples are made whole, and everywhere the
people hear the Word of God.'

He paused for a moment, then went on:

'You are always searching the Scriptures for some light on
the secret of everlasting life. It is there all right, but you don't
find it. You find other things there, many that tell you of my
coming, and those you won't believe. You will not lower
yourselves to come to me for that life everlasting. You will
not deign to show me honour, and indeed I don't desire
honour from you or any man. That is for God only. But I
come in His Name, and you have decided not to receive me
... because you have no love of God in your hearts. How can
you love God when you remain so proud and arrogant –
Pharisee praising Pharisee, Sadducees standing together –
against God – having for God and His Word no praise, no

love, no loyalty? If you really believed the wisdom Moses left you, you would understand, for he wrote to warn you of my coming.'

All this had been said before important members of the Sanhedrin and some of the most learned Rabbis in Israel. The great teachers were impressed, though reluctantly, for they considered themselves the source of all authority as to the Law. They spent their days in disputations to define to a hairsbreadth every possible interpretation of it. So they resented the criticisms of this unknown young man, though he certainly knew the Law very well, and interpreted it with wisdom and understanding. They recognized that much, but would not accept what he said because he had no official standing. He had not studied with them, nor with any other famous teacher, so they asked rather sulkily:

'Where did you learn all this?'

'God speaks through me,' Jesus replied simply. 'I do not speak on any authority of my own. Anyone who has studied the Scriptures should be able to see that. You believe in the Law Moses gave you, but you don't keep it, or you would not be wanting to kill me.'

'Who wants to kill him?' they muttered. 'He must be mad!'

'There is a clause in the Law which says that all who work on the Sabbath should be put to death,' Jesus reminded them. 'There is also a law about circumcision being performed on the eighth day of a child's life, even if that day should be a Sabbath. Do you not suppose that if a child can be circumcized on the Sabbath without breaking the Law, a man's whole body may also be healed on the Sabbath?'

One day after the Passover, when Jesus was back in Galilee, he went to dinner with a Pharisee. While they were still at table, a fine lady from Jerusalem came into the room, with bangles tinkling and a whiff of perfume floating about her.

She had heard of Jesus and was curious to see what he was like, but not interested in his teaching. She walked round the table with a light proud step and head held high, till she came face to face with him. Then suddenly her self-possession deserted her. Their eyes met and she was overwhelmed with shame and remorse. She ran to him, fell on her knees and bowed her head right to the ground before him. Tears streamed from her eyes and dropped on to his bare feet. She took handfuls of her fine dark hair for a towel, and wiped them away. She kissed the feet over and over again as she dried them. She brought a small flask of a very expensive unguent out of her pocket, broke the neck, and poured the ointment over his feet, rubbing it in gently, and continuing to kiss them and to weep.

The Pharisee was scandalized. She was a Sadducee, a lady and rich, but known to be careless of her virtue. He half rose to order her out, but hesitated, expecting Jesus to do so. But as Jesus gave no sign of wishing her to go, the Pharisee felt a sort of malicious triumph.

'If he was really a Prophet,' he thought, 'he'd have known

what sort of woman she is, and he would not have allowed her to so much as touch him!'

Jesus glanced at him and said,

'There's something I want to put to you.'

'Yes?' said the Pharisee.

'It's this. If two men owed money to another, and one owed, say, five hundred pounds and the other only fifty ... and then the man decided to let them both off, knowing that neither had the money to pay with ... which, do you suppose, would be most thankful?'

'Why, the one who owed most and was forgiven it, surely,' replied the Pharisee.

'Yes,' Jesus said, looking down at the woman. 'Look at her, my friend. When I came into this house, I was not offered water to bathe my feet – but she has bathed them with her tears, and used her hair for a towel. I was not welcomed with a kiss, but this woman has kissed and kissed my feet. No one brought ointment for my head, but she has anointed my feet with sweet oil. Her sins are many, but they are forgiven because she has love in her heart. Those to whom little is forgiven, love little.'

He bent over the woman and said, 'Your sins are forgiven.'

The other guests had fallen silent, and his words were heard by everyone present. 'Your faith has saved you.' He added, 'Go in peace.'

CHAPTER 17

SIGNS OF THE TIMES

JESUS took his twelve chosen men on a long tour towards Tyre and Sidon, to get away for a while from the crowds in Galilee and the animosity of the Pharisees, but even there crowds followed him everywhere.

One day when he had gone into a house to rest, to be by himself for a while, a non-Jewish woman, a Greek, came in search of him. She had a daughter who was subject to fits and she begged him to go home with her and cure the child.

'It is not right to take the food meant for children and give it to the little dogs under the table,' Jesus said. 'The children should be fed first.'

She understood at once that he was saying that the children of Israel had first claim on him, but she replied quickly, 'Yes, Lord, but the little dogs get the crumbs which children let drop from their plates.'

Her quick wit made Jesus smile. 'Well said!' he replied. 'Go home. Your daughter is cured.'

The woman ran home, and it was as Jesus had said. The girl was lying on her bed, perfectly well.

It was about this time that a deputation of Pharisees and Sadducees came to ask Jesus for a sign, proving him to be what he claimed.

'You can read the skies,' Jesus said quietly. 'When it is red at sunset, you know that a fine day will follow. And when the sky is red in the morning, you take warning that bad weather lies ahead. Can't you also read for yourselves those more important signs, the signs of the times? Only people who have no faith ask for proofs, and I must tell you that nothing of that kind will be shown you – unless, if you understand it, the sign of Jonah.'

These men, like all Jews, always knew the Scriptures though they understood them so badly. They knew Jonah had been a not very important prophet who had been sent to show a sign of impending doom to the people of Nineveh, who were supposed to be the wickedest on earth. But nevertheless, at Jonah's sign they had repented.

The deputation gave no indication that they had understood, and Jesus turned his back on them and walked away with his Apostles, saying to them, 'Beware of those people. Don't let their lack of faith affect you.'

He said, 'Beware of the *leaven* of the Pharisees' – meaning their influence, working like the leaven or yeast spreading through the dough in breadmaking. Some of the Twelve can't have been listening very attentively, for they thought Jesus was referring to the fact (which they had just remembered) that they had brought no bread with them.

'O you of little faith!' he cried, half laughing at them. 'Why worry about bread? You can't have forgotten so soon how the five thousand were fed. I was not speaking of bread, but of the teaching of the Pharisees and Sadducees and how it spreads among the people.'

They presently came north again to Caesarea Philippi, and there Jesus asked the Twelve who people supposed him to be.

'Some think you are John the Baptist risen from the dead,' one replied.

'Herod thinks so,' another added.

'Some say you must be Elijah, or Jeremiah, or at least one of the old Prophets.'

There was a silence, and then Jesus asked quietly.

'And who do you think I am?'

It was Simon Peter who answered, blurting it out – with absolute conviction.

'You are the Christ, the Son of the living God.'

'Blessed are you, Simon,' Jesus said, 'for no one could have told you that, and you cannot have said it of yourself either. Only your Father in Heaven could have put those words into your mouth.'

It was a wonderful moment. One of them had at last found ears to hear.

'Peter, you are my rock,' Jesus said. 'On such faith I can build, and the gates of hell shall not prevail against it.'

He warned them not to talk about what had happened, nor to tell anyone yet that he was indeed the Christ.

From that time on he began to warn them of the things that the Son of man would have to suffer.

'Jerusalem will have nothing to do with him,' he said. 'He will be rejected by the Elders and the Chief Priests and the Rabbis. He will be killed, but he will rise from the dead on the third day.'

These were terrible things to hear. No one could believe

that the Messiah, the Son of God, in whom all power lay, could possibly be rejected and killed. The idea was inexpressibly painful and frightening. These twelve – these eleven – good friends who had been with Jesus constantly for over a year, were shaken to the heart by it. What shadow of a hope could there be for Israel if he was denied and set at naught? They all knew Isaiah's words, but had never thought about them in relation to the Messiah, certainly not in connection with Jesus:

'He was despised and rejected of men, a man of sorrows and acquainted with grief. He was despised and we esteemed him not. He was wounded for our transgressions, bruised for our iniquities. The chastisement of our peace was upon him, and with his stripes we are healed. All we like sheep have gone astray, we have turned every one to his own way, and the Lord has laid on him the iniquity of us all. He was oppressed and afflicted, and he opened not his mouth. He is brought like a lamb to the slaughter. He was taken from prison and from judgement, and who shall declare his generation, for he was cut off out of the land of the living: for the transgression of my people was he stricken.'

Every single one of the Twelve had known those words from his childhood up, but not one of them had understood them. Not one of them had ever dreamed that they would come true, and about someone they knew and loved.

Peter could not bear it. He caught his arm, and cried out in horror, 'Don't say such things, Lord! You shan't be killed if I can help it.'

But Jesus' face was stern as he said 'Get behind me, Satan.'

Peter could not see that he was playing the part of tempter, that if he could save Jesus from this suffering, it would be against the will of God, and at the cost of leaving the world without hope.

'Anyone who comes with me,' Jesus was saying, 'will have

to deny himself worldly things. He will have to take up my burden and walk in my shadow. Those who try to keep their lives for their own pleasure will certainly lose them, but whoever is ready to lay down his life for my sake will live it to the full. What good would it be for any man to win the whole world, if he also lost his soul? Could he find anything in all his wealth, sufficient to buy back the soul he once had?

A week later Jesus took Peter, James and John away by

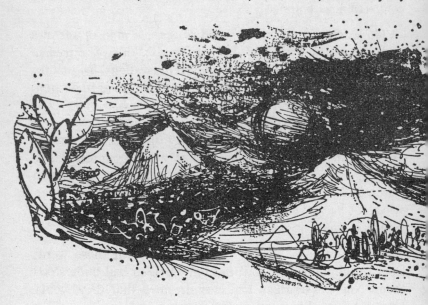

themselves, to a remote place in the mountains. As they stood together it seemed to the three Apostles that light shone through and about Jesus' garments with a blinding whiteness. He seemed to be talking to two men, whom they recognized as the great representatives of the Law and the Prophets; that is Moses and Elijah.

'Master, it is good for us to have been here,' Peter said, 'and if it is your wish, we will build three altars on this spot, one for you and the others for Moses and Elijah.'

'This is my beloved Son. Hear him'

While he was speaking a cloud came down and enveloped them, and each of the three heard in his heart the voice of God saying, '*This is my beloved Son. Hear him.*'

They prostrated themselves, burying their faces in the ground in deepest reverence. Then they felt Jesus laying his hand on each of them in turn, and heard his voice telling them to get up. 'Tell no one what you have seen this day,' he warned them. 'Say nothing until the Son of man has come back from the dead.'

They had already forgotten what he had said about rising again on the third day, and asked one another quietly what 'coming back from the dead' could mean.

Then one of them said, 'The Rabbis say that Elijah has to come back from the dead before the Messiah comes.'

'Elijah certainly comes first,' Jesus replied, 'to prepare men's hearts – but in fact he has already been here, and you know what they have done with him.'

They realized then that he referred to John the Baptist.

They moved on to Capernaum then, and when they reached the house where they were going to stay, Jesus asked the Twelve what they had been arguing about along the road. The answer was slow in coming, because it had been which of them was the most important, and ought to rank first, who second. With Jesus looking at them, it sounded unbelievably silly, and they turned their heads away, ashamed.

'Those who want to be first,' Jesus said, 'come last. To be first always means to be responsible for others, to be every man's servant.'

There were children playing round the door, and he called a little boy over and lifted him on to his knee.

'You can have no part in the Kingdom of Heaven unless you are willing to come to it like children, with simple hearts and eager, open minds. It is a dreadful thing to corrupt a child, and to put stumbling-blocks in the way of a child's faith. It would be better for a man to be thrown into the sea with a millstone round his neck than to be guilty of that. Take care you don't fall into the habit of despising children.'

He let the boy run back to his playmates, and went on talking to the Twelve.

'What do you think?' he asked. 'If a man has a hundred sheep and one of them is missing, will he leave the rest to go in search of it? Don't you think he would? And that he would rejoice when he had found it and brought it back safely to the fold? Don't you think its return would give him greater pleasure than knowing that ninety and nine had never strayed? It is so with the Father. The Son of man has come to save just those lost sheep. It is not by the will of the Father that any one of them is allowed to perish.'

While they were in Galilee, Jesus tried again to prepare the Twelve for the fate that he saw ahead for himself, but still they could not believe it. Only Jesus understood how little hope there was of the High Priests and the Elders, or the Pharisees, listening to him, still less of their being willing to set aside their whole inflexible system for the simple truths which he brought them. Yet he knew that the simple truths would and must prevail, and that he would continue with the task he had been given right to the very end, searching unceasingly for means by which God's purposes might be successfully accomplished.

At this time and on for the rest of his life, the Rabbis and Pharisees laid traps for him wherever he went, trying to trick him into saying or doing things which they would be able to use against him, or which could provoke a crowd to kill him.

CHAPTER 18

THE FEAST OF TABERNACLES

AFTER the Passover, the Feast of Tabernacles was the most important in the Jewish calendar, and the happiest. It was a thanksgiving, for the harvest, but more especially for the fulfilment of God's promise in giving them the land of Canaan. It lasted eight days.

Jesus had not been back in Jerusalem since that stormy scene with the Elders in the Temple, when they saw that he had recognized their desire to kill him. He was at home in Nazareth when most people began to set out, and his family thought he ought to be going too.

'You go on,' Jesus told them. 'For you, it doesn't matter. No one is plotting against you – but there are those who hate me because I have shown them how evil they have made the world.'

They were puzzled, but they set out without him, and later Jesus took one of the unfrequented paths over the hills and walked by himself, unnoticed to the city.

He faced a crisis, between himself and the Elders. He could not change the life of the nation unless he could stir the conscience of those who ruled it, but that he intended to attempt during this Feast.

Meanwhile the Temple had scouts out watching for him. They hoped to catch him before he entered the gates, but one after another the scouts came back with no news of him, and the question, 'Where is that man?' was heard everywhere.

In the outer courts of the Temple there was a constant buzz of excited whispering. People kept their voices low for fear of finding themselves under suspicion of being one of that man's friends.

It was not until the Feast was well started that Jesus arrived, alone, walking openly through the narrow streets. The Court of the Women was crowded with famous teachers engaged in argument and disputation. Jesus sat down among the speakers, and began to teach.

Many of the pilgrims knew nothing of what was going on, but the Jerusalem folk had heard enough to foresee excitement. When Jesus took his place, there was silence, though people were murmuring, 'Isn't that the man?' and 'Is it true they want to kill him?' and 'It takes courage to sit there teaching, with trouble brewing.'

Many wondered that no one interfered with him, and questions were popping on every side.

'Is that the Messiah?'

'Can he be? Really?'

'What do the Elders say?'

'Don't they know?'

Would the Elders want to kill him if he was the Messiah? Did they? Was he? No one knew. He impressed them, but he was not what they expected the Messiah to be. Why, they knew all about Jesus, his parents, and where he came from, even the trade he had followed. The life of the Messiah should have been shrouded in mystery.

As so often, Jesus seemed to reply to their thoughts.

'Yes,' he said, 'you know me and where I come from, but as to how I came and why, you know nothing. I am here because I was sent, and by One who has all authority to send and to command.'

That silenced them for the moment, then the whispering went on. 'When the Messiah comes, will he do more than this man has done?' and the Pharisees began to move. They sent for the Temple guards.

It was not often that Pharisees and Sadducees agreed; they stood for such different things. The Pharisees were narrow, hard, bigoted, but always in the *name* of religion. The Sadducees were scoffers, with little real belief. But they were at one in regarding Jesus as dangerous, which meant that both the central authority in Jerusalem and the widespread control of the Pharisees were solidly against him.

Part of the ceremony of this feast consisted of a libation of water, poured from a golden ewer with the sacred trumpets sounding, in thanksgiving for rain, as a symbol of the stream of love from God towards His people.

Jesus stood up, and cried:

'If anyone thirsts,' – and he meant *thirsts after righteousness* – 'Come to me and drink!'

There was a gasp of surprise, then the voices were heard again.

'He must be the Prophet who was to come!'

'The Messiah! The Messiah!'

'No, no, not the Messiah! He won't come out of Galilee.'

One or two men repeated obstinately, 'The Messiah will come from Bethlehem. It says so in the Scriptures, from the line of David. This man comes from Nazareth in Galilee.'

Hardly anyone in the whole country knew that Jesus had in fact been born in Bethlehem, and he did not enlighten them.

People in the crowd began to quarrel about whether Jesus was the Messiah or not. Some men pushed forward as though to attack him, and the Pharisees and Elders sent to find out what had happened to the guards. One after another of them replied, as though it was excuse enough, 'I never heard anyone speak like that before.'

'Have you fallen under his spell too?' they were asked. 'You ought to know better. None of us believe in him, and that should satisfy you. Fancy letting yourselves be influenced by this rabble, who know nothing of the Law – and will be damned anyway.'

Then Nicodemus – the man who had come to Jesus at night during that first Passover, stepped forward and said, 'But our law does not condemn a man unheard.' He was still afraid to support Jesus openly, but hoped to delay action on this point of law.

'What, are you one of his countrymen?' he was asked. 'Think again! When did a prophet ever come out of Galilee? Never! And never will!'

At evening, the great ceremonial candelabra were lit in the Temple, and their golden glow from that high point could be seen all over the city. Jesus went and stood beside one of them and again called to the people.

'I am the light of the world! Come with me, and walk in darkness no more, but carry light with you wherever you go.'

'Your saying so doesn't make it so,' a Pharisee growled.

'Nevertheless it is so. You can believe me. I know the source of my light. I know where I came from and whither I shall go, and I repeat to you, I do nothing of my own power. My Father is with me and it is He that speaks through me.'

'And where is this father of yours?' they demanded.

'You evidently know Him as little as you know me, or you would recognize me and so find your way back to Him.'

But it was no use. No sense of truth, no love, no urgency touched their hearts or their understanding. To Jesus it was a grievous sight, for they were bringing the whole nation down with them – 'the blind leading the blind,' as he had said earlier.

'I shall leave you soon,' he continued, 'and you will die in your sin. You will try to find me and will not be able to.'

'Do you suppose he is going to commit suicide?' they murmured. 'Is that why we shan't be able to find him?'

'You have so dug yourselves into the earth, that all you care for now are the material things,' Jesus went on. And you will die in your sin. If you cannot believe that I am what I am, you cannot escape.'

'Who are you then?' – but they asked only in mockery. How could Jesus answer them? He did not mean what they did by that title of *Messiah*.

'I am what I have always told you I was,' he said. 'But it is useless to go over that again now. I have still much entrusted to me by the Father to say to you.'

Even then they did not realize that he was speaking of God – though if they had, they might have reckoned it the blasphemy they were waiting for.

'Too late you will know for yourselves that I am what I say,' Jesus continued sadly. 'Too late – when you have lifted up the Son of man.'

A few fell at his feet at those words, penitent, believing. Others half believed, as people who say, 'Oh yes, I expect it is so . . .' but do no more about it.

'Take this thing *into your lives*,' he begged. 'Don't let it slip through your hands. See what it really means, become my true disciples. You will find in it truth, and truth will set you free.'

But that suggestion that they were other than free pricked their pride, for they gloried in having known the freedom of being God's chosen people, who had experienced freedom in conquest, and in slavery, through the freedom of the spirit.

'What do you mean?' they called out angrily. 'We're children of Abraham. We have never been slaves.'

'All who sin are in fact slaves,' Jesus replied, 'slaves to their own weakness. Yet slaves can be freed. It is not a matter of blood with them. They are not part of the family as sons and daughters are. If the Son frees them, they are free indeed.'

As for being children of Abraham – if it was still to mean anything, the *covenant* between God and Abraham must be truly kept and honoured.

'You are searching for a way to kill me,' he told them, 'because you cannot bear the truth which I have been sent to show you. How do you reconcile that with the covenant God made with Abraham?'

'Nevertheless,' they replied, 'children of Abraham we are, and nothing can change that.'

'Then live worthily of Abraham,' Jesus replied. 'The way you are living now suggests a very different father.'

'We have one father – God,' they retorted. 'We were not born in sin.'

'Ah, if God was really your Father, and you loved Him as you say night and morning, with all your heart and soul, you would have felt some of that love for me also, for He sent me to you. But neither God nor Abraham is truly your father. You are children of the devil, who has been a liar and a murderer from the beginning of time. You will not accept me because what I have brought you is the truth. Can any of you deny it?'

He waited, but no answer came.

'Then, if what I have said is true – and none of you have denied it – why do you not believe me?'

Why should they believe him? Nothing could ever make them less than God's children. They always had been, always would be, God's chosen people. Nothing could change that.

'Children of God recognize truth when they hear it,' Jesus went on. 'You are not children of God.'

No one ever questioned that but the Samaritans.

'So that's it!' the Elders cried triumphantly. 'You're a Samaritan – and mad!'

'I am not mad,' Jesus replied. 'Believe, oh, believe me, those who accept my words shall never see death.'

He did not mean that they would never die, but that death would no longer be an absolute end, with no hope beyond it.

'Oh, he's mad!' they cried. 'Of course he's mad. Abraham is dead. So are the Prophets. They're all dead – but he says we shall never die if we follow him! Who do you think you are?' they shouted. 'One greater than our Father Abraham?'

'Father Abraham himself exulted in the prospect of my coming,' Jesus said.

'You are not fifty yet,' they threw back at him, 'and you speak of Abraham – dead more than a thousand years – exulting in your coming!'

'Yet I tell you truly,' Jesus replied, 'I was in existence before even Abraham's day.'

This was the point to which he had been carefully leading them. If what he had said was not the grossest blasphemy, it should, from their own knowledge of the Scriptures, have forced recognition from them.

Jesus had argued with them, hoping to reach some point they would have to recognize and accept, but not one word went home. What they were after that day was blasphemy. Only for that they heard him.

The Temple guards had not returned, and that was perhaps

to the good, for they might have intervened. Death by stoning was accepted, and there was plenty of ammunition, as the builders had only stopped work for the Feast. Summary execution would have suited the Elders, relieving them of responsibility.

There was a silence, then men stooped with the swiftness of hot indignation and clear decision. They picked up great lumps of masonry – and Jesus' life, in the ordinary course of events, would have ended there and then. But his work was not finished, and man cannot in the end prevail against God. For a few moments there was chaos while men shouted and stones flew, but Jesus walked out of the Court untouched, as he had done on that hillside in Galilee when men wanted to make him king.

CHAPTER 19

THE MAN BORN BLIND

A WEEK later Jesus was walking in the part of Jerusalem farthest from the Temple when he heard the cries of a blind beggar who always sat at the gate there, wailing for alms.

'He was born blind,' one of the disciples remarked. 'Was that punishment for some sin of his own, or for something his parents did?'

'Neither,' Jesus said, 'but in order that some special work of God may be wrought, and as long as I am here, I shall bring light and carry out God's works.'

He spat on the ground (saliva was considered good for the eyes) and making a little paste with the dust, he spread it over the man's eyes. As it was the Sabbath, he was breaking the Law, both in mixing the paste – which was 'work' – and in applying it to the eyes. Then he told the man to go and wash in the pool of Siloam near-by and he found he could see.

The beggar did not return to his pitch, but went home, and as he approached, neighbours looked up in surprise. They were accustomed to see him groping along close to the wall; now he was stepping out boldly like other men.

'Isn't that the beggar who sits by the Dung gate all day?' someone asked.

'Yes it is,' the man called out, 'I am the blind beggar,' but his words were drowned in a shower of questions about how it happened.

'The man called Jesus did it,' he told them. 'He made some clay and put it on my eyes, and told me to wash in Siloam, and I did, and now I can see.'

They rushed him off to the local Synagogue Council where

he was questioned by Pharisees. They were not the clever men of the Temple, not so experienced in getting at the facts. The beggar repeated his story just as he had told it to the neighbours.

'But it's the Sabbath,' the Pharisees objected, 'that man can't come from God if he does not keep the Sabbath.'

But some members of the Council hesitated.

'Could a bad man do such a thing?' they wondered.

The spokesman then turned back to the beggar and asked what he thought of the man who had given him his sight.

'He was a prophet, I'm sure,' he answered.

This annoyed the Pharisees, and they said he probably was not blind in the first place. Beggars always made themselves look worse than they were to wring money out of passers-by. So they sent for his parents.

'Is this your son?' they asked when the old couple arrived. 'Is it true he was born blind?'

'Yes,' they answered nervously. 'He's our son, and he has always been blind, right from the day he was born.'

'Then how is it he can see now?' demanded the Pharisees.

They could not say. 'Ask him,' they quavered. 'He's old enough to speak for himself. Let him tell you.'

They knew that they might be expelled from the Synagogue if it was thought that they were followers of Jesus, and they were afraid.

The Pharisees turned back to the beggar and, with the formal phrase, 'Glory be to God!' began to argue with him.

'Now to begin with, we know the man's a law-breaker.'

'I don't know that,' the beggar interrupted them. 'All I know is that I've always been blind, and now I can see.'

'What exactly did he do?' they demanded. 'How did he open your eyes?'

'I've told you that once,' the man cried. 'Why do you want it repeated all over again? Didn't you listen? Or are you going to be his disciples?'

That made them angrier, and they shot back at him, 'You're probably one yourself. That must be it. We're followers of Moses – that's good enough for us. No one can doubt that God spoke to him – but this fellow! No one really knows anything about him.'

'That's a fine thing!' cried the beggar. 'Here's a man who

could give me *sight* – *me, born blind* – and you say you don't know anything about him! Why it's never been heard of before, a man being given his sight after being born blind, but that's what he did. That's something to know about him, and he could not have done a thing like that without God's blessing. You're always saying God won't listen to sinners. Well, there you are! This man can't be a sinner.'

He was so excited by what had happened to him that he did not care for all the Council's threats. He simply stuck to what he knew to be the facts.

The Pharisees were disgusted.

'You were in sin before you were born,' they threw at him. 'Don't you try to teach us what is right,' and they drove him out of the building, but did not expel him.

Jesus heard what had happened, and went after the man.

'My son, how much faith have you?' he said to him. 'Do you believe in the Son of man?'

'Who is he, Master?' the simple man replied. 'Tell me so that I may know.'

'You have seen him,' Jesus said, knowing how few men the beggar had seen in his life, 'he is speaking to you now.'

'O Master, then I believe,' he said.

To the people who were watching, Jesus said:

'I have observed this world since I came into it, and I find that there are blind men who see, and many thinking they see who are really blind.'

There were Pharisees among the crowd, and one asked haughtily, 'You're not suggesting *we* are blind, are you?'

'No blame would attach to you if you were blind,' Jesus replied. 'The trouble is that you say you see, and if you see, you sin with your eyes open, and that is guilt indeed.'

They resented very much being called blind by this man who constantly and openly broke the Law, and had no satisfactory authority for what he did. This was the second time he had referred to them publicly as 'blind'.

To show what he meant, Jesus then told them a story about the differences between devoted shepherds and the hirelings who did no more than they were paid for – meaning those who truly cared for Israel, and those who merely served their own interest.

When flocks were brought in from the hills at night, they used to be shut up in a courtyard or cave near where the owner lived. Their own shepherd brought them in and saw that they were safely penned. When he came back in the morning, the sheep got up at the sound of his voice, ready to follow him out again, for they knew him. Sometimes several flocks spent the night in the same fold, each brought by its own shepherd. No thief could come through the door – only the real shepherds had the key. So the thief would have to climb over the wall, and that would not give him much chance of getting sheep away quietly.

Sometimes hired men had to be sent out with the flock, but they were never so reliable as the real shepherds. It took a lifetime of patience and devotion to learn their craft, working day after day with the sheep till each one was known and each came to know and trust him. If wolves or a lion attacked the flock, the hireling would fly for his life and leave the sheep, but a good shepherd would stay and face the danger, even if it meant death for him.

This little talk was heard with satisfaction, for most of the listeners knew from their own experience how true it was, but its inner meaning escaped them. The Pharisees, however, turned away angrily, muttering, 'He has a devil. He's mad. Why do we waste our time listening to him?'

To which there was a faint murmur of 'He doesn't sound mad to us, and would a devil give sight to a blind man?'

CHAPTER 20

THE GOOD SAMARITAN

AFTER the crowd in the Temple had tried to stone Jesus and failed, it was evidently decided to wait until there was enough evidence against him to satisfy the Romans. The Jews could not, as a matter of fact, carry out the death sentence without getting it ratified by the Romans, but they did not want the responsibility for his death to rest directly on themselves. If they could put up a charge of sedition, it would have to be dealt with by Rome in the ordinary course of events. So to get the necessary evidence they sent spies after Jesus wherever he went to listen and note all he said.

There were things Jesus had still to do however. Above all he had to ensure that he left behind him such understanding of the Gospel as would keep it alive, after his death, for all time. He left nothing in writing, no letters, diaries, notes, or any book. All depended on the minds and memories of the men he had chosen to instruct.

There were plenty of witnesses of the deeds he had done, the miracles of healing, the great works such as the feeding of the five thousand – but men might come to dispute them, to pretend they never happened, or that the people must have been deceived. But his great teachings must be remembered, and he repeated them, now in one way, now in another; and later eleven of the Apostles pieced them together and made what were really eye-witness chronicles which they repeated every day and passed on to others by word of mouth. In that time of few books, memories were strong and accustomed to retaining a great deal with absolute accuracy – which was fortunate for us.

'Blessed are the eyes which see what you look on,' Jesus told them one day. 'Prophets and Kings have longed to see them, and to hear what you have heard. Let these things sink down into your ears.'

But none of them was able to take his warning, no one really understood what he was telling them.

For the next part of his work Jesus required more messengers and began to choose men to make the twelve up to seventy. But as it turned out, not all he chose were willing. One said his father was dead and he really ought to go home for the funeral. Another had bought a piece of land and needed to get back to see about it. A third thought he would like to go home and say good-bye to his parents.

'When a man sets his hand to the plough,' Jesus told them, 'he knows he has to go on to the end of the furrow.' But he let them go, and selected others in their place.

'Wherever you go, I'll go too,' a man cried eagerly, but Jesus shook his head. 'The birds of the air have nests, and the foxes holes,' he said, 'but the Son of man has no resting-place.'

However, he found seventy men who were willing, and gave them instructions which were much the same as had been given to the twelve on their first journeys alone, but this time the work was not to be confined to Israel's lost sheep. They were to go to Gentiles as well, and particularly to Samaria. They were not to preach, but only to announce that Jesus was on his way. They were not to loiter, for time was short. They were not to take anything with them, food or extra clothes. And again Jesus warned them that he was sending them out on a dangerous task.

'But whoever listens to you, will hear me,' he told them. 'Those who won't receive you, reject not you but God.'

James and John, who always did things together, were sent to Samaria – Jesus greatly desired to see the feud between Samaritans and Jews ended – but as they began to talk about him in one village the people rose angrily and drove them out. They had heard of what had passed in Jerusalem, and felt that Jesus had taken his stand with the Jews, and deserted them. The brother Apostles were taken by surprise and went indignantly back to Jesus and wanted him to let them call down fire from heaven on the village and its people.

'O children!' Jesus cried, 'does the spirit you are made of mean so little to you? The Son of man is not here to destroy men, but to save them.' But Samaria had to be left until a later date, when Peter led the Apostles; and the whole country as a man accepted the Gospel.

Soon after this they went down over the hills to the Jordan, and crossed the river into Perea. The people who lived on the far side had not heard or seen Jesus and he and the seventy were kept very busy. One day, when they were near the ford across which the road to Jerusalem ran by way of Jericho, a Rabbi stopped them and asked:

'What shall I do to enter the Kingdom of Heaven?'

It was a question many people asked, but this time it was put by one whose whole life was devoted to the study of the Scriptures.

'You know the Law,' Jesus replied. 'What do you suppose it means?'

The Rabbi replied, 'That I should love God with all my heart, with all my soul and mind, and with all my strength. And that I should love my neighbour as myself.'

'Well said,' Jesus agreed. 'Keep those two laws and you will earn your place in the Kingdom.'

But the Rabbi did not care to be dismissed so easily, and began to argue,

'Ah, but who is my neighbour?'

From where they were standing they could see the line of the twisty switchback of a road up to Jericho, with the bare rocky hills on its far side, honeycombed with caves in which brigands hid, ready to swoop on passers-by, and Jesus said:

'A man was going down that road one day when he was set on by robbers. They half killed him, took all he had, even his clothes, and left him naked and bleeding under the hot sun. A priest came along, saw him and crossed over to the other side of the road, and went on his way without a word. Another man from the Temple came by, and he did the same. Then it happened that a Samaritan on an ass came along. He saw the man and dismounted. He went over and looked at him, fetched flasks from the ass's back and poured wine over the wounds to clean them, and oil to heal them. He tore up his shirt to make bandages and when he had bound him up as well as he could, he lifted him on to his beast, and walked on to the inn, holding him on the ass's back. He put him in charge of the landlord and brought money out of his pocket to pay for his keep and for anything extra the landlord might have to buy. Which of the passers-by do you think was his neighbour?'

'Oh, the one who went to his assistance,' said the Rabbi.

'Yes,' said Jesus, 'and that is what you have to do.'

While they were still in Perea, which was part of Herod's territory, some Pharisees came to Jesus and, pretending to be his friends, warned him to go away. 'Herod wants to kill you,' they said. 'Fly for your life.' But they were mocking him, hoping he would run away, and look foolish.

'Go and tell that fox,' said Jesus, 'that today, and tomorrow too, I shall continue to heal and cast out devils. On the third day my work will be done, but during today and tomorrow things must take their course – and on the day after that also. A prophet cannot perish outside Jerusalem.'

The men went away feeling small, for their trick had fallen flat, and Jesus cried in a very different tone, 'O Jerusalem! Jerusalem! Killing the prophets, and stoning those who bring you God's word! How often have I longed to gather your children together, as a hen gathers her brood under her wing, but you would not.'

CHAPTER 21

THE PRODIGAL SON

AGAIN on a Sabbath, Jesus was asked to a meal with important Pharisees, and noticed how the other guests made straight for the best seats, those nearest the host, and he said:

'When you go to a wedding, remember that people more important than yourselves may have been invited too. Let your host choose those he wishes to honour, while you take your seats at the lower tables. Then, if he misses you, he will stand up and say, "My friend, come up here and sit with me." But if you have put yourself at his right hand, and he has to ask you to move down and make room for someone else, you will feel slighted and ashamed before the company.'

To his hosts, Jesus then said:

'When you invite friends to a meal, don't think only of your family and friends, or of people who will ask you back. Invite those who can make no return – the poor, blind and crippled. You will find it brings unexpected blessings.'

One of the Pharisees' guests then remarked, 'Those who sit down to a feast in the Kingdom of Heaven must be blessed!'

'Yes,' Jesus said, 'yet many have been invited who will not be there. They find all kinds of excuses for refusing, and the poor and the sick – who you think are not fit to be asked to this table – will be brought in to the places of honour!'

If these things did not please the Pharisees, there were others present who liked the sound of them, and when Jesus left the house a number of them went after him. Jesus turned round and made clearer what he had been saying.

'If anyone wants to follow me,' he said, 'if you want to come into the Kingdom of Heaven with me, you have to be ready to put the Kingdom before everything else, even your own family and friends, even before your own life. And you have to count the cost, just as you would before starting to build a house. No one in his senses starts to build without first getting an estimate and seeing that he can afford it. It is a bad business all round to get as far as laying the foundations, and then to have to abandon it for lack of money. It's the same when you start to choose righteousness and to build your path to the Kingdom.'

All through Perea, numbers of 'publicans and sinners' flocked to hear Jesus and they were in earnest, eager to hear what he was teaching, and quick to apply what he said to themselves. But everywhere the Pharisees looked on in grim disapproval, for Jesus never condemned men they considered almost public enemies. He talked to them as he talked to the Pharisees themselves, and if they were penitent, he exacted no penalties but said 'Sin no more'. He tried to explain to the Pharisees why that was right, and again used the familiar parallel of sheep which most of them owned.

'If any of you lose a sheep,' he said, 'you know you will go out and look for it until you find it, leaving the rest of your flock in their safe folds. You would go right out into the desert after it if necessary, and you don't kill it when you find it as punishment for its having strayed, you are so pleased that you carry it home in triumph and shout to your neighbours to tell them it is safe. It's exactly like that with the Father and the sinners who have strayed from the safety of the fold. I tell you, there is joy in heaven over one sinner who is brought back. Did you ever hear the tale of the Prodigal Son?'

Then he went on to tell them about a man who had two sons. The elder was faithful and hard working, but the younger could not settle to anything, and one day he said to his father, 'When you die, I suppose you will leave me part of all you have. Give me my share now and let me go away.' His father was sorry, but he gave it to him, and the young man departed and had a riotous time in foreign cities. He enjoyed himself until the money was spent. Then it happened that the crops failed in that country and there was a famine. He tried to get work, but men were being turned away. He left the city and walked out into the open places where there were farms, thinking that there would surely be work there, and food to be had. But all he was offered was a job as swine-herd. By then he was so down and out he would even have eaten the pigfood. Hungry, penniless, and alone, he thought a great deal about his home and his kind father.

He thought how foolish he had been. There was no one working for his father who did not get enough to eat. Gradually he felt really sorry and made up his mind to go home and say so. 'I can't expect him to take me back on the old footing,' he thought. 'I grabbed my share of all he had and came away and wasted it. Still, he might let me work in the fields. I'd work hard for him.'

So he set out, and a long, weary way it was. At home, his father often went up into a turret and looked over the land-scape straining his eyes to search for him. At last, while the son was still a long way off, the father saw him. He called to the servants to get water ready, and to bring a good coat and shoes. He told them to kill the calf that was being fattened, and to prepare a feast of welcome – 'For my son is coming,' he cried. 'I thought he was dead, and he is alive.'

The elder brother was at work in the fields and did not return until evening, when he heard sounds of merrymaking, and smelled the cooking. A servant told him what it was all about, and he was so angry he would not go indoors.

The old man went out and pleaded with him to come in and welcome his brother, but he refused. 'Look at all the years I've worked for you,' he said, 'and you've never given me so much as a kid to entertain my friends with. But first you give him half of all you had, and now that is spent, you welcome him back like a king!'

'Son,' the father said gently, 'you stayed with me, and all that I have is yours. But it is right to rejoice that the boy has returned to us and is alive and well. I feared he was dead.'

Two or three Pharisees came to Jesus one day and asked derisively:

'Well, and how soon now will you be setting up that kingdom of yours?'

'The Kingdom of Heaven is not like that,' Jesus replied. 'It will never be seen so that people can point to it and say, Look, there it is!'

The Kingdom begins within you, like the seed in the earth and you are in fact already part of it. It is wherever the Son of man is at work. It had therefore been right in the midst of these very Pharisees all the time Jesus had been with them. But by their own choice they remained outside, refusing to accept it.

'The time will come,' Jesus ended, turning to his own disciples, 'when you will long to call back one of the days of the Son of man, and it won't be possible. Beware then when you hear people say they have seen him. His days are like a blaze of lightning out of the sky, lighting up the earth for a moment, then gone. But before that happens, he must endure. He will suffer, he will be denied, and utterly rejected by this generation.

'Looking back,' Jesus went on sombrely, 'it will seem as though the days of the Son of man were like the time when Noah was building the Ark. People still went carelessly about their ordinary business, never dreaming, not believing, that the flood was so near, though they had been warned. It was so near indeed, that they were caught in it, overwhelmed by it, and drowned – while Noah and all who went with him into the Ark were saved.'

At Bethany

The cold rainy season was in full swing when they came
up the steep, twisting road from Jericho to the Mount of
Olives, which was two miles outside Jerusalem. There was a
pleasant little village among the olive groves called Bethany,
and there Jesus turned aside. The woman who had anointed
his feet in the Pharisee's house at Capernaum lived there
with her sister Martha, and her brother Lazarus. Jesus did not
want to go straight to Jerusalem, and as he entered the village
Martha met him and brought him to their home.

For Jesus, that home was a haven of rest; quiet, gracious

and full of happiness, and the sisters and their brother were eager listeners.

That day at the Pharisee's house Mary had met the great crisis of her life, and had made a choice from which she never looked back. It had made her a different person, though she was still light and graceful, charmingly dressed and delicately perfumed. Martha was the practical one, attending to all the household business, yet anxious too to have time to listen to Jesus. Lazarus was a man to whom Jesus could open his heart and his mind, and it was a joy to him to do so during that short space of time.

Martha went out to the kitchen to see that everything was being well prepared, and a room got ready for Jesus. They could hear her voice as she sent the servants hither and thither. Yet through it all, she wanted to get back to listen to Jesus, and soon returned complaining that Mary was not doing her share.

'Is it right for her to leave everything to me?' she demanded. 'Tell her to come and lend me a hand.'

'O Martha!' Jesus must have smiled at her. 'Don't fuss and fret so about these things. There are others that matter more – one specially, and that Mary has chosen. It must not be taken from her.'

'Oh well,' Martha said, and went out, still grumbling, but satisfied too, for she and Mary were devoted sisters.

Between the ridge of the Mount of Olives on which Bethany stood and the high eastern walls of Jerusalem lay the Kidron Valley. Behind the walls, the city was spread out on the rise of the Holy Hill, aslant, almost as if it could slide off into the valley beneath. And on the summit stood the Temple, catching the first flashing rays of the early sun on its great doors and gilded wall.

The Feast of the Dedication – only a few days away – was a feast of thankgiving for the cleansing of the Temple after its desecration by the Syrians. It was not one of the occasions when everyone was expected to go to Jerusalem, but Jesus intended to be in the Temple during the eight days of its celebration. He went alone and, as it was cold and wet, took shelter under the colonnade of Solomon's Porch and walked about there, with his cloak wrapped round him for warmth, thinking, meditating, praying.

Suddenly there were people about him asking:

'How much longer are you going to keep us in doubt? Are you, or are you not, the Christ, the Messiah? Give us a plain answer that we can understand.'

Jesus went up alone to Jerusalem

Jesus replied to them slowly, 'I have told you already – but you see you did not believe me.'

It would have been useless to try to prove such a thing to their satisfaction, for the fact was that they and Jesus did not mean the same things by the words they used. Jesus had already put before them all the evidence of what he was and why he had come – if none of it convinced them, they were not of his flock.

'What I have done in God's name witnesses to me,' he told them. 'But you have not recognized my voice, you will not follow me – you are not my sheep. Those who come to me as their shepherd recognize me, and they will be safe with me. No wolf will be able to snatch them out of my hands, for my hands are the hands of the Father. I and the Father are one.'

Again, this was supreme blasphemy, or divine revelation, and these people had not even a moment of doubt. They ran for stones, crying 'Death to the blasphemer!'

Unafraid, Jesus stood his ground, facing them. 'I have done the Father's good work for you all to see,' he said quietly, 'for which of them do you stone me?'

'Not for your deeds, but for the words you have just spoken,' they declared hotly. 'You made yourself out to be God.'

'There is a Psalm,' Jesus said, ' *"Ye are gods, and all of you are children of the most High".*'

The men paused – and dropped their stones.

'If I have not performed the works of God, don't believe me,' Jesus went on. 'But if I have, believe *them* even if you won't believe me, so that you may come to see that the Father is in me, and I in the Father.'

But at that they turned on him again and tried to rush him before them into the Council Chamber of the Sanhedrin, but in the scuffle, they lost him and he went away.

He left Jerusalem, and did not return to Bethany, but went on to the Jordan, close to where John the Baptist had first proclaimed his message, *Repent, for the Kingdom of Heaven is at hand.* There Jesus taught for a while, and people came from far away to hear him. Many believed in him, and were heard to say:

'John performed no miracles, but what he said of this man was true.'

CHAPTER 22

THE RAISING OF LAZARUS

SINCE his baptism Jesus had performed six 'works' which were of special importance. The first was when he turned water into wine at the wedding feast at Cana.

The second made visible the power of faith, when he healed the little son of one of Herod's stewards.

The third was the healing of the paralysed man at the pool of Bethesda.

The greatest sign of all was the feeding of the five thousand.

The fifth was Jesus walking on the water to save the disciples.

The sixth showed him as the world's light, when he gave sight to the man who had been born blind.

But the moment had come for the seventh to be performed, and this was perhaps the greatest of them all: partly a lesson in faith, and partly a preparation for what was to come, for happenings that would make terrible demands on the faith and the love of the chosen Twelve. But above all, it was a mighty act of power.

Jesus was still in the Jordan valley, twenty miles from Bethany, when Lazarus was suddenly taken mortally ill, and his sisters sent out a messenger to find Jesus and tell him so.

When he heard the news Jesus said, 'This sickness is not unto death. It is a means by which God may be glorified.'

Some of the disciples must have remembered what he had said about the man who had been born blind, but they appeared to take his words literally, meaning that Lazarus was not desperately ill.

Jesus had grown to love each member of that family at Bethany, yet he stayed away from them for another two days, and Lazarus died about the time he received the message.

When those days had passed, Jesus announced that he was going back to Judea. He did not speak of Bethany, and the disciples were afraid for his safety. One of them cried, 'O Master! To Judea? After they have twice tried to stone you?'

'A day has twelve hours,' Jesus replied, 'and while the light lasts men do not stumble. It is in the darkness of the night when there is no light to guide them that they trip and fall.'

He wanted them to understand that he had still a little time left in this world, and that nothing could happen to him or to them until the right moment, the moment in which God gave His consent.

Then he said, 'Lazarus our friend has fallen asleep. I go to wake him.'

Peter, James, and John had been present when Jesus used those words of Jairus's little daughter, but another of the disciples said:

'Master, if he's sleeping, it ought to do him good.'

'He is dead,' Jesus said plainly, 'and I am glad I was not there – *for your sakes*. It may be that you will learn more about faith this way.'

Thomas thought he meant that, with faith, they could run into danger without fear, and said briskly, 'Very well, let us all go and die with him.'

The Jordan valley at that point lies more than 1,200 feet below sea level, and is hot and airless. It was a stiff climb to Bethany, more than twice that height above them, but the air freshened as they strode on. Outside the village Jesus stopped and sent one of the disciples forward to tell the sisters where he was. Many Sadducee families lived there, and he did not want to attract their attention.

At that moment Lazarus had been lying more than three days in the rocky cave which was his tomb, and friends from Jerusalem were paying visits of condolence to the sisters. So many came that Martha was kept busy preparing refreshments, and it fell to Mary to receive the visitors. It was therefore Martha who took Jesus' message, and she immediately dropped what she was doing, and ran out just as she was to find him.

'O Master!' she cried, 'if only you had been with us, he would not have died. I know your Father in Heaven gives you anything you ask for.'

'Lazarus will rise again,' Jesus told her.

'At the Last Day,' Martha agreed, unconsoled. 'Yes, I know that.'

The Pharisees believed in life after death, but not the Sadducees. Her family were Sadducees, but she had learned that much.

Jesus then spoke the words which have become part of the service for the burial of the dead.

'I am the Resurrection and the Life. He that believes in me will live, even though he dies. And whoever believes in me while he is alive, shall never die. Can you believe that?'

The words were difficult, and Martha did not reply to them. She said simply,

'I have always believed that you were *he who was to come*, the Messiah, the Christ, the Son of God.' And she turned away as Jesus asked her to send Mary to him.

She hurried back and beckoned Mary out of the room crowded with their melancholy guests.

'The Master is here, near the tomb, and wants to see you,' she whispered.

Mary did not hesitate either, but ran out at once, as Martha had done, and went as quickly as she could to Jesus. Their visitors thought she must have gone to wail at Lazarus's tomb, and after a while they followed her.

When Mary reached Jesus, she fell at his feet, and like Martha, cried, 'O Master if you had been here, my brother would not have died.'

The sight of her intense grief for Lazarus distressed Jesus. She wailed as women did in that country for the dead, and the guests, who were on their way towards her, heard the sound and raised their voices also.

Tears ran down Jesus' face, and sorrow shook his whole body but he put personal feelings aside for the act of God he was about to perform.

'Where have you laid him?' he asked presently, and several people pointed to the mouth of the cave.

'He must have loved Lazarus very much,' someone said as they all moved nearer.

Another person recognized him as Jesus of Nazareth, and said, 'Would not you have thought that the man who made that blind beggar see, could have saved their brother?'

But the seventh sign was being wrought. Jesus was racked by the intensity of his prayer and by the power that was moving in him. It was clear to them all that he was enduring a tremendous strain.

'Move away the stone,' he said at last, but Martha the practical one, who had now joined them, cried out in horror.

'Lord! He's been dead four days! The cave will be stinking!'

'Remember,' Jesus said, 'I told you if you had faith you would see the glory of God's power.'

The disciples went forward to do as he had said, and rolled away the flat round millstone which closed the tomb.

Then, so that all who were present should know that what

was about to happen was being done by God, Jesus said aloud, 'Father, thank you for having heard me,' and, in commanding tones he called, *'Lazarus! Come out!'*

The dead man came out, his hands and feet still swathed in the burial cloths, and a napkin about his head.

'Free him from those things and let him go home,' Jesus said.

Some of those who had witnessed this miracle were convinced by it, and accepted Jesus as the Son of God. Others went back to Jerusalem and told what they had seen to members of the Sanhedrin. They were alarmed and called on the High Priests, who summoned an emergency meeting to consider what to do. They had been afraid of something of this kind, remarkable enough to fire the people.

'What are we doing?' various members demanded. 'If we let this man go on, he'll carry the nation with him. Then we shall have Rome descending on us, and they will make an end of us here in the Temple, and wipe us out as a people.'

Caiaphas, the High Priest, broke in cynically,

'Let's face it. It will be much more convenient to have that one man killed, than for the whole nation to perish.'

Thus was the High Priest inspired by God to make that prophecy in the Temple, that Jesus should die for the sake of the people.

From that moment their plan to kill him took positive shape, and they set a price on his head, offering a reward for his capture, dead or alive.

Jesus therefore did not linger in Jerusalem. He could not go about openly among the people, so he went away to a little town high up in the Judean hills, alone, with the Twelve and some more of the seventy following him separately to escape notice.

CHAPTER 23

THE LAST JOURNEY

E PHRAIM stood more than two thousand feet above the deep valley through which the Jordan ran, a dark serpentine thread, twisting and coiling its way through the mud. The worst of the rainy season was over, though it would continue mildly until the end of April. Through the damp and the mire, bands of pilgrims from the north were soon moving slowly along the low road. At night their camp fires made a smudge of smoke, shot through with an occasional gleam of fire.

No sound came up to their retreat, but Jesus and his disciples knew that as those men from Galilee plodded on by day they would be singing the Psalms they all loved so well, the same in which Jesus had joined so expectantly twenty years ago when he went with Joseph and Mary to keep the Passover of his coming of age in Jerusalem. He had made the journey many times since then. He had often sung those Psalms. His memory held them, as it held so much of the Scriptures.

They were singing 'I will lift up mine eyes unto the hills', and 'O pray for the peace of Jerusalem!' and 'If it had not been the Lord who was on our side when men rose up against us, they had swallowed us up whole.' They sang, 'As the mountains are round about Jerusalem, so the Lord is round about his people.' They sang in triumph, 'When the Lord turned again the captivity of Zion, we were like them that dream, our mouth was filled with laughter, and our tongue with singing. Then said they among the heathen, The Lord has done great things for them. . . . He that goeth forth weeping, bearing precious seed, shall doubtless come again with joy, bringing his sheaves with him.'

What were the pilgrim band expecting of their Passover in Jerusalem? What were they, in fact, going up to see? Among them were almost certainly men Jesus had healed. Some must have heard him teaching in Synagogues or on the hillsides. Had they believed in him? Or had they listened to the Pharisees? Not one of them dreamed that, before they kept the Feast, Jesus would have been tried, condemned, and executed.

Soon Jesus himself left the heights and started down, knowing what he meant to do, knowing there was a price on his head, yet going to join the throng. He too was going to Jerusalem for the feast. He walked ahead of his disciples, alone, and they, staring at his back, were afraid. He felt their fear, turned and drew them about him, to share with them what was in his mind, to prepare them for what now lay immediately before them. But still they could not accept it.

'We are going to Jerusalem,' he told them, 'and this will happen there. The Son of man will be handed over to the High Priests and condemned to death. He will be delivered to the heathen, to the Romans, who will hold him up to scorn. They will spit on him. They will lash him with their whips. In the end they will kill him. They will crucify him.'

The Twelve were aghast, but still held it impossible. All they had come to believe seemed to mean something so different.

'But on the third day he will rise,' Jesus added quietly.

Even John, whom Jesus loved so dearly, did not understand. He and James pressed forward, asking eagerly, 'When you come into your Kingdom, Lord, will you have us to sit beside you, one on your right and the other on your left?'

'What are you asking?' Jesus replied. 'Do you think you can drink the cup that waits for me? Can you be baptized with what I have to undergo?'

'Yes,' they said.

They were thinking of kings with thrones of gold – he of

an ordeal to be endured in absolute loneliness. They were to see very soon two men placed one at his right hand, one at his left, but they would not be his disciples.

'You shall drink that cup,' Jesus told them gently. 'You shall undergo that baptism – but the seats on my right hand and on my left are not mine to give.'

The other ten were furious at the presumption of the brothers, but Jesus restrained them.

'Our Roman rulers are proud,' he said, 'and you know how they use their power over the weak. It must not be so with you. You must learn greatness through humility. If you would ever be master, you must know what it is like to be a slave. Even the Son of man did not come to be served and waited on, but himself to minister to others, and to ransom his people with his own life.'

They went on in a knot, walking close together, still on a crest of the hills, going towards the road which ran down between the borders of Samaria and Galilee. Jesus had no fear. He knew with absolute certainty that nothing and no one could forestall or prevent what was to happen in Jerusalem, for that was the will of God, and he went down openly and joined the pilgrims, walking among them, talking to them, trying even now to lead them into the right fold.

When they came to the outskirts of Jericho there were two blind men by the wayside, begging. One was called Bartimaeus. They heard the noise of the approaching pilgrims, and called loudly for alms. Someone told Bartimaeus that Jesus was there, and he shouted, 'Jesus, Son of David, have mercy on us!'

Some of the disciples, not as confident as their Master, told them to be quiet. They did not want attention drawn to him. But the blind men only shouted more clamorously, 'Son of David, have mercy on us!'

Jesus stood still, and asked the disciples to bring them to him.

'Cheer up,' they said. 'He's going to see you.'

'What do you want me to do?' Jesus asked.

'Give me my sight,' said Bartimaeus.

'Go on your way then, your faith has gained it for you,' Jesus said.

'Pray,' Jesus said to his disciples. 'Pray constantly, and never lose heart. God will hear you. But pray humbly, never think yourself better than other people because you are on your knees. Don't be like the Pharisee, who found himself in the Temple with a tax collector, and stood where he could be seen, praying aloud, thanking God that he was not like other men. "I don't drive hard bargains," he boasted to God, "or cheat, or run about after women. I'm not like that tax collector over there, Lord. I fast regularly twice a week, and always give away a tenth of my income."

'But the tax collector was so conscious of his sins that he stayed at the back, out of the way, with eyes downcast, and only cried despairingly within himself, "O God, I'm such a sinner, have mercy on me!" '

Mothers with children began to come out of the procession of pilgrims to bring their children to Jesus for his blessing. The disciples did not want him to be worried, and tried to keep them away, but Jesus called out,

'Don't stop children coming to me. They are already in the Kingdom. It is only by coming to it as children that the rest of you will enter.'

Hearing those words, a young man of considerable wealth and position came forward and asked how he could make sure of entering the Kingdom.

'You know the commandments,' Jesus said. 'Do not commit adultery, do not kill, or steal, or lie. Honour your father and mother.'

'Yes, yes,' said the young man, 'I've always kept the commandments.'

'You are rich,' said Jesus. 'Sell all you have and give to the poor – you will find treasure in heaven.'

At that the young man turned away. Jesus' words made him very sad. He couldn't give away all he had.

'It is hard for the rich to find their way into the Kingdom,' Jesus observed. 'A camel might more easily get through the eye of a needle!'

That idea took the people round him quite by surprise, and they protested, 'Who can be saved if not the rich?'

'We left everything, Lord,' Peter said uneasily, 'home, family, and livelihood, to follow you.'

Jesus nodded to him. 'And no one who has given up home, family, and livelihood for the sake of the Kingdom shall lack reward even in this world. In the next he shall have life everlasting.'

The long train of pilgrims had now reached Jericho, which was to be their last camp before they came to the outskirts of Jerusalem. The stretch of road which lay ahead was the dangerous one Jesus had described in the story of the good Samaritan. Even in a crowd, they would not risk camping along it. Jericho was an important place with a Roman garrison, palaces, and a hippodrome built by Herod. It was on the main caravan route to Damascus, and had a busy customs post where a good many tax collectors worked. It was also the home of many priests. About half the priests lived in or around Jerusalem, and most of the rest came out to Jericho, so pilgrims of any position in the world were pretty sure of a night's lodging there. That was not the kind of lodging Jesus chose. Even now that his days were numbered, he was busy on that work entrusted to him for the lost sheep of Israel.

So it happened that when he came upon a rich tax collector there, he spent the night with him. The man's name was Zaccheus. He was head of the customs post, with men working under him, and much hated by other Jews because he had lowered himself to work for the Romans.

He had heard of Jesus, and when he discovered that he was among the Passover pilgrims who were entering the town, he determined to have a look at him. He was a little man who could never see anything in the middle of a crowd, and Jesus was always surrounded by masses of people, so he climbed a tree and watched as they passed by.

Jesus saw him and called, 'Come down out of that tree, and hurry up! I want to spend the night with you.'

Zaccheus scrambled down in delight, but those about Jesus raised a howl of protest. Surely he could find a more suitable place to stay for the night? If he was really a man of God, would not any priest welcome him?

But there before them all, the tax collector made a vow.

'Lord, hear me,' he said. 'This day I will give half of all I possess to the poor, and I will repay fourfold anything I have ever taken wrongly from any man.'

'Salvation has come indeed to your house this day!' Jesus remarked, and added to the crowd, 'Zaccheus is also a son of Abraham – and one of the lost sheep I came to save.'

The pilgrims climbed the long sultry gorge next day to the slopes of the Mount of Olives, some to camp there, some along the Kidron Valley. Near Bethany Jesus left them to spend the Sabbath with his friends.

He arrived at Martha and Mary's house a little before sunset – that is before the Sabbath had begun. When it was over, the sisters arranged a supper to which they invited guests. People kept coming in and out to look at Lazarus – the man who had come back from the dead. Preparations for the meal kept Martha busy as usual.

All through that, his last Sabbath, Mary was aware of something strange and sorrowful about Jesus, and she too was very quiet and withdrawn. She had a terrible sense of foreboding. She shed no tears now, for she had no concern for herself. She was feeling out with all her heart and soul towards the deep sadness which wrapped Jesus about like a cloak though his face was not hidden and his eyes saw all that went on.

Mary had enjoyed the gay, luxurious things of life, elegance and admiration. She had lived carelessly, and her sins, as Jesus had said, were many. But all had been forgiven on that day when she fell at his feet in sorrow and remorse, washing them with her tears.

She had discovered then a different kind of love, her whole heart was filled with it to overflowing, and not only her heart, but her good mind as well, her insight and penetration were all in it, loving, praying, trying to comprehend what Jesus, in silence and loneliness, was enduring.

Then quietly she went out of the room and returned with another flask of ointment, of fine alabaster, lovely as a gift for a king. In the stillness she broke the neck of it and poured the perfumed cream over Jesus' feet, smoothing it in with her hands, finishing it off with her long hair, and the scent was wafted out, all over the house.

An angry voice broke the spell, and there was Judas glowering at her from the doorway, demanding:

'What are you doing? That could have been sold for a good price, and the money given to the poor.'

He also was going through a dark hour, for he had plans of his own.

'Let her alone,' Jesus said wearily. 'You will always have the poor to care for, but not me. Let her keep the rest to anoint my body for burial.'

Judas hardly glanced at him, and slunk out again. Jesus knew he was not thinking of the poor.

In Jerusalem, the High Priests and Elders were eyeing one another speculatively, and asking: 'What do you think? Will he come for the Feast?'

Next day Jesus left Bethany and went to meet his enemies,

knowing that between themselves they had already condemned him to death, and were interested only in finding some easy way to trap him.

He prepared deliberately to enter the city as the prophets had said the Messiah would, not regally like the kings of this world, but humbly, riding upon a donkey. Two of his Twelve were sent to fetch one that had never been ridden, and they put their coats on its back for him.

The pilgrims with whom he had travelled the last part of the way to the outskirts of Jerusalem had spread the news of his arrival, and that he would keep the Passover there. Early in the morning after the Sabbath they began pouring out along the Bethany road in search of him. Jesus soon met them, and as the donkey climbed the hilly path between the two spurs of the Mount of Olives, another crowd approached from Jerusalem, and the two met. The excitement was intense. They had torn down great palm leaves and were waving them in triumph. With wild fervour they shouted. *'Hail! Hosanna to the Son of David! Blessed is the King of Israel who cometh in the Name of the Lord!'*

The noise was deafening, and continued all the way. The road rose again, and turned about a spur of the hill, and in another minute the whole city was spread before their eyes, a city 'compact' indeed, with narrow streets and closely packed buildings, gleaming wet under the grey sky.

'O Jerusalem! Jerusalem!' Jesus cried, as his eyes rested on it. 'You who kill the prophets!'

He allowed these people to hail him as King, and he knew what he was doing. That was necessary to the significance his coming had to bear. He had to enter Jerusalem in such a way that no one should misunderstand his claim was to be the Messiah. All religious Jews, the High Priests and Elders would recognize it, and must then accept, or kill him. There was no other possibility. If he was not the Messiah, he was an impostor, guilty of blasphemy in the highest degree. These

'Hosanna to the Son of David!'

were the things he had foreseen, that was the situation he had brought about.

As he passed, with the acclamation of crowds ringing up between the narrow walls, the people of Jerusalem looked out from their latticed windows to see what was happening, or climbed on to their roofs for a better view. They were surprisingly ignorant, and shouted down to the crowd, 'Who is it? Who is it?'

To which the pilgrims from Galilee replied proudly, 'Jesus the Prophet, from Nazareth in Galilee.'

Even then they only claimed him as a prophet, and their pride was half for their own country. They had not learned enough – or had not courage enough – to proclaim him also within the walls of Jerusalem as the Messiah, the Son of God.

A prophet from Nazareth did not interest the Jerusalem folk. They expected nothing from Galilee. Then Pharisees broke through the crowd to expostulate with Jesus.

'Can't you restrain these people?' they demanded, for the uproar was terrifying.

'If I did, the very stones would cry out,' Jesus replied.

It was necessary to attract attention, so that everyone might be brought to think, if only for a moment, what his coming meant.

Jesus went on and into the Temple. No one tried to stop him, or interfered with him in any way. He walked about, as though seeing that all was prepared for the scenes that were to follow. Then he returned to Bethany.

This is the day Christians remember as Palm Sunday.

In the Council Chamber of the Temple the Pharisees and other members of the Sanhedrin looked very grim.

'We had better not try anything with a crowd like this,' they said. 'Everyone in the world seems to have gone out after him.'

They decided that if they could not dispose of him quietly, they had better not act until the feast was over and the pilgrims had gone back to their own countries.

CHAPTER 24

FOR THE PRICE OF A SLAVE

JESUS spent that night in prayer, fasting, and next morning he returned to Jerusalem. When he and the Twelve reached the Temple, Jesus went to Solomon's Porch where the traders brought their cattle. As he expected, the market was in full swing again, and again he drove them out as he had done two years ago.

'My house shall be called a house of prayer for all nations, but you make it a den of thieves,' he told them.

Considering all that was brewing in the Temple against him, it may seem strange that no one stopped him, but the place was cleared, and as traders and beasts streamed out by one door, sick and crippled came in from another and filled it up again. This was the only time Jesus healed inside the Temple. While he was going round among them making the sick well, and the cripples active, a crowd of children ventured in. They crept up to him, and daringly raised the shout they had heard the day before in the streets.

'Hosanna to the Son of David!'

That brought Temple officers out, and one said to Jesus,

'Do you hear what they are saying?'

'I do,' Jesus replied. 'Out of the mouths of babes and sucklings the Lord brings forth truth.'

The next day, Tuesday, saw many matters brought to a head. Crowds gathered early in the Temple, and Jesus was there to teach them, but one after another representatives of the various factions in the Sanhedrin came out to question, to trap him. The first was a deputation from those who were responsible for what was taught in the Temple, they asked by what authority Jesus was there, and who had given him authority to teach.

'Tell me first what you think of John,' Jesus said, 'did his baptism come from God or not?'

The members of the deputation knew that most people believed without a doubt that John was a great prophet. To deny it before the pilgrims might cause a riot. But if they admitted it, Jesus would certainly ask why they had not believed him. It was not truth that exercised their minds, but only the question of what was expedient, so they dropped their eyes and declined to answer.

Though they were perfectly right to demand the qualifications of anyone who taught in the Courts of the Temple, this prevarication showed quite clearly that they had not come out honestly in their official capacity, but to lead him into a trap.

Jesus turned back to the crowd and told them about Israel as the nation God had trained through the ages as His chosen people. They were His people. He was their King. The men in charge, High Priests and the rest, were God's deputies – and that all good Jews believed quite literally. But these men in charge had acted like dictators, owning no master. They had killed, one after another, the messengers of God, now they were planning to kill His son.

'There was once a man who planted a vineyard,' he began. 'He put a hedge round it, and dug a pit for the wine press. He built a watch tower from which to look over his property, and then he put some men in charge of it while he went out of the country. When some time had elapsed, he sent a messenger to see how the vineyard was doing, and to bring back some of its grapes to show him. But the men set on his messenger and beat him, so he returned to his master sore and empty-handed. The master sent more messengers, some were beaten, some were killed, but no account of the state of the vineyard reached him.

' "What shall I do about these people?" he asked himself at last. "I wonder if I sent my own son whether they would recognize his authority and do what I want?"

'So he sent his son. But when the men saw him coming, they put their heads together and said, "That's the heir. If we get rid of him, we can take over the vineyard for ourselves." So they killed him and threw his body over the hedge.

'What do you suppose the Master of that vineyard would do with those men?' Jesus asked. 'Don't you think it likely that he would get rid of them and hand the place over to other people?'

The Pharisees stood there hiding their anger, for they understood perfectly what the parable meant, but again fear of trouble with the crowd held them back. They went away, into one of the Sanhedrin chambers, and sent out other Pharisees with men who were known to have friendly associations with the Romans. They had a dangerously tricky question for Jesus, and thought he could not help becoming involved whichever way he answered it.

'Master,' they began civilly, 'you are an honest man, and you teach God's truth and nothing else in spite of anything people may say and do, so please give us your opinion. *Is it lawful to pay tribute money to Caesar?*'

There cannot have been a single person present who did not recognize how dangerous the question was. No good Jew ever admitted that Rome had any right to make them pay tribute, but if Jesus denied it – and those friends of Rome heard him – he would be charged with uttering seditious words in the Temple, charged by the Romans, and the penalty was death. On the other hand, if he said that the Roman tax was just, the crowd, for all their admiring attention, might well tear him to pieces.

Seeing their purpose, Jesus merely replied,

'Why do you try to trap me like this? Show me a denarius.'

When one was given him, he asked, 'Whose head is this engraved on it? And what name appears in the inscription?'

'Caesar's,' they replied – both the head and the name.

'Then render to Caesar the things that are Caesar's,' Jesus told them. 'And to God, the things that are God's.'

Almost equally discomfited and astonished, the men turned away, knowing that they had failed.

Some Sadducees came next, very negligent in manner and scoffing in tone, hoping to see Jesus look a fool before the crowd. Their question was about the resurrection, in which they did not believe. It made the Pharisees' ideas appear very silly, but they did not mind that. They despised them.

'By the law of Moses,' they said, 'if a man dies childless, his widow must marry his brother so that an heir may still be produced. If the brother dies, she must marry the next brother and so on as long as there are any brothers left, or until she has produced an heir. She might have to marry seven brothers, one after the other. Then whose wife would she be in the resurrection?'

'You start with the wrong idea,' Jesus replied. 'Can you really be so ignorant both of the Scriptures and of the power of God? When the dead rise again, there will be no such thing as marrying or being married. They will live like angels. As for resurrection, in which you do not believe, you should know at least that when God spoke to Moses in the burning bush, he said "I am" – not I was – "the God of Abraham, and of Isaac, and of Jacob" – not of Abraham dead as dust, but of Abraham *living*.'

The Scriptures being their history, as well as their religion, the Sadducees could not reply to what Jesus had said, without exposing themselves to the people as unbelievers, so they also retired.

Finally came a Rabbi who delighted in argument. He came

not to trap Jesus so much as to inveigle him into a disputation after his own heart.

'Which is the greatest commandment?' he asked, and with the six hundred and thirteen precepts of the Law, there was immense scope for a hair-splitting dispute. But Jesus answered him simply and directly.

'There is no greater commandment than the *Shema, Hear, O Israel, the Lord our God is one, and thou shalt love the Lord thy God with all thy heart, and all thy soul, and all thy mind, and all thy strength.* This is the first commandment, and the second derives from it. *Thou shalt love thy neighbour as thyself.* The whole of the Law, and all the wisdom of the Prophets depend on these two.'

The Rabbi recognized greatness, and said respectfully, 'You speak wisely, Master. What you say is the truth. There is one God and none beside Him. To love Him with all one's heart and all one's understanding, one's whole soul and strength – and to love one's neighbour as oneself – that is more than all the sacrifices and burnt offerings.'

'You are not far from the Kingdom of God,' Jesus said.

All the day's questioners had been silenced, and with truth and wisdom, though it was neither truth nor wisdom that had been sought there that day. The men of the Temple had failed in each attempt to trap him, and the failure rankled. But their intentions were unchanged.

That men occupying such positions of responsibility towards the nation should have stooped to such tricks grieved Jesus, and he said to the crowd:

'Beware of these men. They sit in Moses' seat and teach the Law, but they don't keep it in their own lives. You must learn the Law and obey it as they tell you, but don't look to them for an example. They don't practise what they preach. They lay their heavy loads on poor men's shoulders, with never a thought as to how they are to carry them. Their concern is all for their own importance, and they make a great show of holiness in order that you will show them deep respect and admiration.'

Looking then across to where the Scribes and Pharisees lingered, he went on:

'Woe to you who keep the Kingdom of Heaven locked against the people. You decline to go in yourselves, and refuse to let anyone else past you. You take infinite care to separate out the tenth part of even the small herbs in your gardens for tithes, but ignore the greater matters of justice and mercy and good faith. You wash the outside of the cup which others can see, but you leave the inside dirty. You like to make out that if you had lived in the old days *you* would never have killed the prophets as your forefathers did. But those who killed them were, as you say, *your* forefathers, and you are truly their children.

'O Jerusalem! Jerusalem! See how your house is left desolate, even at the moment when light is on its way through to you out of the darkness!'

Jesus left the city, and Caiaphas the High Priest called a hurried meeting of the Elders in his Palace. Their plans and hopes had miscarried badly. They cursed those cheering crowds in the streets who made it so difficult for them to act.

Then Judas showed his hand. He went to the Palace and got himself admitted to the Chamber where Caiaphas was, and to him he made his offer of help. He was prepared to stay with the Twelve until Jesus was in some isolated place, more or less alone. Then he would creep away and bring Temple officers to arrest him quickly without anyone knowing what was happening.

Caiaphas and the Elders were surprised at their luck. They smiled and accepted.

'But how much will you pay?' Judas added, and they

named contemptuously the price commonly given for a slave, thirty pieces of silver.

Peter, James, John and Andrew were with Jesus when he left the Temple after that long, strange day, and they looked up at the great gates and the huge stones in the walls, taking in their grandeur and richness as though seeing them for the first time. They drew Jesus' attention to them.

'Yes, look well at them,' Jesus answered, 'for the time is not far distant when not one of its stones will be left standing.'

They went out down the stepped zigzag path to the valley, and up the other side to the slopes of the Mount of Olives until they were on a level with the Temple again, with the gap of the valley between them and it. Jesus turned to look back, and sat down where he could go on looking.

'When will it be,' one of the disciples asked, 'that destruction you spoke about just now?'

When the first of the gospels was written – that is, Mark's – the Temple was still standing. But before Matthew and

Luke wrote their books, it had been demolished by the Roman Emperor Titus – and that was in A.D. 70.

Jesus did not answer their question directly. Jerusalem, as the old visible centre of their religion, had been fading and dying for the past six hundred years. Jeremiah had seen that it would happen, when he found the voice of God speaking in his heart. Soon in its place Jesus himself would stand as the new, invisible centre drawing all men to God.

'You will have to be always on your guard,' he said at last, 'against imposters who will claim to be me, risen from the dead. Nation will rise against nation, in pursuit of these false Christs. There will be famines, pestilences, earthquakes – but don't be afraid, even when wars come. And have faith when you are hauled before the Synagogues or the Temple. Endure and survive. When you stand accused, you must bear witness to what you have seen and heard. But don't worry about what you will say. I will put truth and wisdom into your mouths, and your enemies won't be able to deny or dispute it. *Endure and survive*, for the Gospel must be handed on, to all peoples all over the world. Fear, greed, cruelty, and other iniquities will abound – even within each one of you – but the Gospel will spread. It will gain power until at last it conquers and wins. But I warn you again to beware of false Christs. Though heaven and earth pass away, my words never shall.

'Watch and pray, for you never know what one day will bring forth. Do you suppose thieves would get much of a haul if the master of the house knew the hour of their coming? No, for he would set a watch and prevent them. Always be prepared, for the Son of man will come when you least expect it.'

His concern for his little band of brothers was so great that he tried to warn them in one way after another, and to fortify them. They would be left behind as witnesses of all he had done. Their memories held all the records there were of what he had taught and of the things they had seen; but they were untried, so little able to understand even what was happening before their eyes.

Night was coming down on the white stones of the Temple, and the valley was filling with shadows. It was cool and a breeze stirred in the olive groves.

'The Son of man will come again to judge the world,' Jesus said. 'He will sort men, like a shepherd putting sheep and goats into separate pens.'

The freedom to choose is ours, but the responsibility also, and there comes a moment when all have to account for what they have done with that freedom.

'To those he places on his right hand,' Jesus continued, 'he will say "Come into the Kingdom. You fed me when I was hungry, and brought me water when I thirsted. You took me in as a stranger, and found clothes for me when I was naked. You visited me when I was sick, you came to me in prison." They will probably say they never knew me hungry or thisty, or as a stranger, or naked, or sick, or in prison – but whenever you do as much for any wretched creature in the world, you do it to me.

'To those remaining, on his left, he will say, "You that have chosen evil, depart from me into the fire that destroys utterly. You never fed me, or gave me drink, or took me in, or clothed me. You never comforted or helped me when I was sick or in prison." These wretched ones will also cry out that they never saw me hungry or thirsty or naked, and never knew I had been sick or in prison. But the answer is the same. When they chose not to do these things for the wretched and forsaken people in the world, they failed to do them for me.'

Jesus said much more to them before they left that quiet spot; then he went back to Bethany and rested there, over Wednesday, and on until Thursday morning.

Meanwhile the crowds continued to pour in and out of the Temple where, behind the scenes, the plotters were deciding what steps they would take after Judas had led them to Jesus and he was safely bound and delivered. There was much coming and going between the Temple and Caiaphas's Palace.

CHAPTER 25

THE LAST SUPPER

WHEN the Feast of the Passover fell, as it did that year, on a Friday – which would mean having two Sabbaths on end – there were two possibilities. The Feast could be held on the Friday, eaten after sundown and so within the normal Sabbath Day, or it could be held on the day before, the Thursday. The Pharisees, and therefore most Jews, preferred the Friday, but Jesus chose the Thursday. He was, as it turned out, crucified as the animals were being slaughtered in the Temple to provide the Paschal lamb for the feast.

On the Thursday morning Peter and John went to Jesus to learn where he wanted to keep the Passover supper. Bethany, with Mary and Martha, might have seemed natural, for it was counted within the bounds of Jerusalem for such purposes, but Jesus wished to keep it actually in the city, and he told them how to find a large upper room which would be put at their disposal.

'You will find the master of the house carrying in pitchers of water,' he told them.

Much water would be needed that day for cleansing and purification in readiness for the feast, and as water carrying was a woman's job, the sight of a man going to and fro with the heavy pitchers would be sure to catch their eyes.

'Tell him the Master says his time is near, and he wishes to keep the Passover in that house with his disciples. He will show you the room, and you will find there all that is necessary, and you can go ahead and get everything ready.'

They found the house as he had said. The upper room was furnished with a low long table with couches down the long

sides, and another, for three people, across the top. The guests
reclined on the couches, leaning on their left elbows, with
their bodies stretched out at an angle away from the table.
This position was part of the traditional Passover customs, to
remind them of ease after slavery. Peter and John went to
market and bought the flat round loaves of bread, the wine,
the lamb and bitter herbs.

At dusk Jesus arrived with the rest of the Twelve, and
Judas was still with them.

'I have so greatly desired to keep this Passover with you,' Jesus told them, 'for I will not keep another until all is accomplished.'

The Passover was a family feast, and when, as now, a group of friends kept it together, one of them took the place of the father, as Jesus did that night. Where he sat was the centre and heart of the group. There was a little argument as the Twelve selected their places. Peter and John were in so many things Jesus' right-hand men that it probably seemed natural that they should be on either side of him. In fact John did sit on his right, but it was Judas who claimed the left hand, and Peter was displeased. He took the place nearest John, but round the corner of the table.

Jesus had noticed the quarrel and asked, 'Who is more important in your eyes, those who dine, or the one who waits on them?' Not pausing for their reply, he added, 'I am here as servant.'

He rose and laid aside his garments and wrapped a towel about him. He fetched a basin of water and began to wash the disciples' feet, starting at the far end of the table. When his turn came Peter cried out in protest.

'Master, you shall never wash my feet!'

'You don't know yet what I am doing, later you will,' Jesus replied.

But Peter cried, 'No, you shall never wash my feet.'

'If not, you have no part in me,' Jesus warned him, and he gave in extravagantly, crying:

'Then not only my feet, but my hands and head too, Lord!'

'Not your hands nor your head,' Jesus chided him gently, 'only your feet, then you will be clean every bit.' He was silent a moment, then added, 'But not all of you here will be clean.'

He was thinking of Judas. The feeling of that treachery so near him lay heavily on his heart. He finished the washing, pouring the water even over Judas's feet and wiping them carefully with the towel.

'Do always to one another as I have done to you,' he said. 'The servant is not greater than the master, an apostle is not greater than he who sends him out.'

It was plain that he was deeply troubled, and he went on to say, 'I tell you now so that you may be prepared. One of you is going to betray me.'

Eleven of the twelve were simple, honest men. They knew how often they erred without knowing it, now they turned to one another, asking anxiously, 'Can it be me?'

Peter beckoned to John who was in a position to whisper to Jesus, as he could lean back against him and speak into his ear. 'Ask who it is,' Peter said softly, and John twisted round and put the question. Also speaking low, Jesus replied, 'He to whom I shall give the sop when I have dipped it.'

He then dipped a crust of bread into the gravy, and Judas took it.

'What you have to do, do quickly,' Jesus said to him, still speaking so quietly that no one else realized what was going on. But Judas knew then that Jesus had read his mind, and he got up and went out. The other disciples thought he must have been sent to buy something that was needed – more bread perhaps, or wine – and the meal went on.

Presently Jesus took the bread and blessed it, broke it and passed it round to each of his disciples. '*Take and eat,*' he said, '*for this is my body.*'

He took the wine and blessed it also, passing it to them and saying:

'*Drink you all of this, for it is my blood of the new co-venant, shed for many for the remission of sins.*'

For himself he refused it, saying, 'I will drink no more of the fruit of the vine until I drink it new in the Kingdom of God.'

He did not ask them to share his burden of sorrow, but

tried to find words of comfort to help them through the ordeal which was going to be so hard for them to bear. It was their last chance of hearing his words, though they did not know it.

They sang together then, the Great Hallel, the Passover Psalms, among them one which said, '*The Lord is on my side: I will not fear what man can do to me.*'

'My children,' Jesus said, 'I shall be with you only a little longer. You will search for me after that but, as I told them in Jerusalem, where I am going you cannot follow. This I want you to do for me: *love one another*. Love one another as I have loved you. If you love one another, that will show the world that you are my disciples.'

'Where are you going, Master?' Peter asked uneasily.

'You cannot follow where I am going, Peter,' Jesus replied.

'Why not?' Peter demanded, though he began to fear that Jesus was speaking of death, 'I would die for you.'

'Would you, Peter? Would you die for me? Before cock-crow you will deny knowing me three times over.'

Peter, aghast at the idea, was silent.

'Let not your hearts be troubled,' Jesus went on, 'trust God and trust me also. In my Father's Kingdom there are many resting-places. If it were not so, should I have said I would prepare a place for you? You know the road by which I shall travel.'

'How can we know that, Master,' asked Thomas, 'if we don't know where you are going?'

'I am the road,' Jesus said. 'Only through me, only by me, can you go to the Father.'

'Show us the Father then, and we shall be satisfied,' said Philip, as though Jesus was speaking of material things like maps and books and incense smoke.

'You have been with me throughout these two long years,' Jesus said. 'Haven't you recognized me yet? When you see me, you have already seen the Father. Don't you believe that I am in the Father, and He in me? The words I speak are not mine. The things I have done were not mine. The Father gave me the words, and wrought the works through me. If you love me, you will remember what I have taught you, and I will ask the Father to send you another Comforter, the spirit of truth, to strengthen and fortify you, and to be with you evermore.

'I cannot talk to you much longer; come, let us go on our way.'

They left the lighted room with the remains of the feast and went out into the moonlit darkness, across the Temple Court and past the great gateway where the golden vine, so cunningly wrought, trailed its gilded branches in the full beam of the moon.

'I am the vine,' Jesus said, looking up at it. 'My Father is the husbandman. Barren branches that bear no fruit have to be cut away and the pruning makes the rest bear better. I am the vine, you are the branches.'

But the branches can bear neither leaves nor fruit unless they remain part of the vine, open, so that the sap can run through them to the tipmost bud.

'Again and again I beg you to love one another,' Jesus went on. 'When you find yourselves hated by the outside world, remember they hated me too. Remember that if they persecuted me, they will persecute you – but remember also that if they observed my word, they will observe yours. I warn you of such things so that when they happen you will remember what I have said. I should like to say much more . . . but you could not bear it now. Only be sure that I came forth from the Father, and now when I leave the world, I shall return to Him.'

'Now you speak plainly, and we really believe you are from God,' said several of the disciples.

'At this moment, yes,' Jesus warned them, 'but very soon

you will scatter and leave me alone – though not alone, for the Father will be with me. I have said these things that in me you may find peace. In the world you will have tribulation enough. But be of good cheer, *I have overcome the world.*'

Presently Jesus asked them, 'When I sent you out with neither money nor provisions, nor even shoes, did you ever lack anything?'

'Nothing,' they replied.

Jesus nodded. 'Times have changed now. You will need all you have – even swords.'

'We've got two here, Master,' Peter cried eagerly.

He was ready to risk his life fighting, but that was not what Jesus wanted.

As they went down into the Kidron Valley Jesus gave them another warning.

'You will all falter this night because of me. When the shepherd is attacked, the sheep scatter. But after I have risen, I will go before you into Galilee.'

'Master, though everyone else falter, I never will,' Peter cried impetuously.

'This very night, Peter, before the dawn watch, you will deny me three times over.'

'Even if it meant dying with you, I wouldn't deny you,' Peter cried more passionately than before, and the rest of them joined in, declaring that they would never desert him.

So they came, climbing a little way, to a garden of olive trees which is called Gethsemane. There was an inner garden, walled round, and Jesus left most of them at the gate outside it, saying to them, 'Stay here while I go and pray.' But yearning for companionship and understanding, he took Peter and James and John with him.

As they stood together in the moonlight among the trees, Jesus murmured, 'My soul is sorrowful, even unto death. Stay and keep watch here.'

He went a few paces from them, and prostrated himself on

the ground, praying to be shown God's will even at that last moment.

'Father,' he prayed, 'all things are possible to Thee. Take this cup from me ... but not if Thy will is I should drink it.'

He came to that hour of agony, as in the Temptation after his baptism, human and divine, feeling no inspired certainty of the path he had to take, groping for it with complete human feeling within his divinity, making his choice, believing that what he chose was God's will. But if it should not be God's will, he might be bringing to naught God's whole purpose for the world. All had been put into his hands, but he had to find the means whereby the end might be achieved.

He suffered in the full knowledge of all human pain, of ignominy and malicious cruelty, knowing the terrible endurance that would be demanded of him: knowing even the agony of uncertainty.

Satisfied at length that the will of God was truly flowing through him – like the sap through the vine – he rose and went back to his friends for a brief moment of comfort in their closeness. But they had not been with him in spirit. They were not even watching for his safety. They were leaning against one another, asleep.

'O Peter, sleeping!' Jesus sighed. 'Could you not watch with me one hour?' Then, as Peter opened heavy eyes, Jesus besought him, 'Watch and pray for your own sake, lest you fail in the hour of trial. Your spirit is willing I know, but the flesh is weak.'

He went away again, and prayed in the same words as before, racked with anguish, and again he rose reassured, and went back to Peter and James and John. But again they slept. A third time Jesus left them, still not wholly certain that he had chosen aright. A third time he prayed in agony for guidance, and this time rose to his feet, strong and resolute,

'Do you betray me with a kiss?'

knowing that he had truly found the will of God. Knowing also that if it was God's will, he would find, put into his heart by the Father Himself, all the courage and endurance he would need to bear what it involved.

'Never mind now,' he told his disciples, 'get up. Let us go and meet them.'

They heard at that moment the sound his ears had caught already – the approach of many feet – and they saw the glow of lanterns and torches round the walls. Men came through the gate nervously, waving their weapons. A detachment of Roman soldiers had accompanied the Temple officers. A step ahead of them came Judas. He had known that Jesus would take the Bethany road and stop at this place, and he had recognized the group of disciples waiting outside. The garden was a safe place to capture Jesus, and Judas went to him, crying 'Master, Master!' and kissed him on the cheek so that there should be no doubt as to whom they were to arrest.

'Judas, do you betray me with a kiss?' Jesus said, and then to the men, 'Whom do you want?'

'Jesus of Nazareth,' they replied gruffly.

'I am he,' Jesus replied.

Peter did not at once realize how many there were, and cried, 'Master, shall we fight?' He drew the sword he had boasted of earlier, and struck out at the man nearest him, slicing off his ear – thereby putting himself in considerable danger.

'Put up your sword,' Jesus said instantly, and he touched the man's ear and healed it. 'Do you think I would refuse what the Father has set me to do?'

Men from the Temple went quickly to his side, and as they bound his hands behind him, he said, 'If it is I you seek let the others go.' And the disciples, seeing what was happening, ran away.

Jesus was hustled out of the garden, and faced the rest of the crowd, who were waiting for him. Elders and Scribes from

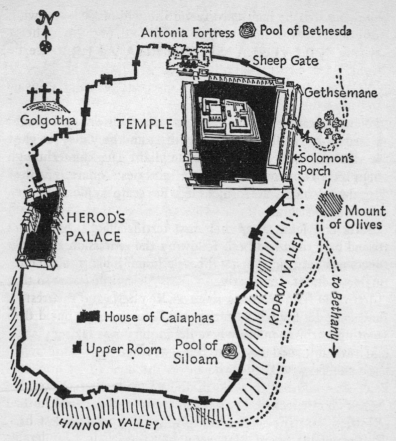

PLAN OF JERUSALEM

the Temple had come to see him arrested, some with clubs in their hands, and some swords.

'Why do you come for me as though I was a bandit?' Jesus asked. 'You saw me in the Temple every day this past week, teaching, and made no attempt then to take me.'

CHAPTER 26

TRIALS AND BETRAYALS

IT was nearing midnight when the men dragged Jesus roughly up that familiar path from the valley of the Kidron, with jeers and triumphant laughter echoing about him. They took him to the High Priests' quarters in the Temple, to Annas, the former High Priest, to decide upon the charge against him.

Peter and John, after their first terrified flight, had soon turned back, and had been following the procession at a distance, not yet ready to stand beside Jesus in his trouble, but unable to desert him utterly.

John had friends among some of the priests and their families, so he got himself admitted, but Peter was shut out. John went up to the chamber where the inquiry was taking place, and realizing suddenly that Peter was not with him, went back and persuaded the woman on the door to let him in. Peter was allowed to wait in the courtyard on to which Annas's house looked. The woman knew John as one of Jesus' followers, and she looked sharply at Peter and exclaimed. 'You're not another of them, are you?'

'No,' Peter said quickly and, shivering with misery and fear, he went over to a brazier where a fire was burning.

Annas questioned Jesus about his disciples and what he had taught, hoping to find something which might suggest that he had been training young men as rebels against Rome. But he had no right to try to make a prisoner incriminate himself, as they both knew, and Jesus replied:

'Why do you ask me? I have always taught openly in the Synagogues and the Temple. I have done nothing secretly. Ask those who heard what I said. They know what I taught.'

Annas should have had witnesses there, for as well as against, the prisoner, and that was what Jesus was telling him. One of the Temple police who thought he was being impertinent, slapped him sharply and said:

'Don't speak to the High Priest like that.'

It was not legal either to strike a prisoner, and Jesus said,

'If I do wrong, it is your business to give evidence to that effect. But you should not strike me.'

Annas realized that he was making no headway, and sent Jesus on to Caiaphas, who was the reigning High Priest.

It was now after midnight and the actual day of the Passover Feast, so Jesus had either to be kept in prison for at least three days, over Friday and the Sabbath, on to Sunday: or he must be tried, sentenced, executed, and the body taken away before six o'clock that same evening, a matter of something less than eighteen hours. If he had to be kept in prison three days, the crowds of pilgrims were sure to hear of it, and might protest. Caiaphas therefore intended to rush the trial and see that Jesus was dead before sundown.

Jesus was taken across the courtyard where Peter was still crouching by the fire. A few members of the Sanhedrin were present and some witnesses, but it did not amount to an official gathering. In any case it was against Jewish law for a man to be tried on a capital charge before daylight. They were only going through the motions of a trial, however. The sentence had been pronounced weeks before, on that day after Jesus had raised Lazarus from the dead. All they needed now was a charge which the Romans would accept without question.

The spies who had been employed to watch Jesus during the past weeks had returned, with plenty to say, but no two of them told quite the same story, and it was essential to have two witnesses agreeing absolutely if their evidence was to be accepted.

Witnesses to the scene in the Temple when Jesus had

driven out the traders were also called, but again no two agreed on the exact words he had used. The Chief Priests thought they might have had a case against him as a sorcerer if he had said he would destroy the Temple and set it up again by magic. That would have discredited him completely, and incurred the death sentence. Or there was just a chance of interpreting it as an instigation to rioting, to destroy the Temple: and that would be an easy matter to get the Governor to accept.

Jesus listened to the malicious voices and was silent. No gibes, no lies of theirs produced any change of expression. Then, in exasperation, Caiaphas said to him, 'Have you nothing to say about all that is being witnessed against you?'

Jesus made no reply. There was nothing in it for him to answer; and that Caiaphas knew too.

In the end the High Priest was obliged to put the question he most wanted to avoid. With all the solemnity his office entitled him to assume, he adjured Jesus,

'By the living God, tell us whether you are the Christ, the Son of God?'

Now that the real issue had been raised, Jesus replied.

'If I tell you that I am, you will not believe it. If I ask you what you mean by "Christ", you will not tell me. Whatever I say, you will not release me.'

Some of those present spat at him. The men holding him pulled his cloak over his eyes, hit him, and cried, 'Now, Prophet, say who struck you!' Even servants pushed forward to hit him.

Outside, in the courtyard, Peter's face was also hidden in his cloak, yet a passing servant cried, 'That's another of them!'

'I'm not!' Peter shouted, but a man standing near him said, 'Well, you speak like a Galilean.'

At that Peter began to bluster, cursing the man, and swearing that he had never set eyes on Jesus.

In the brief silence that followed, he heard the trumpet sound for the end of the watch called Cockcrow, which had lasted from midnight till three a.m. After that hour the Jews could legally pass sentence and they took Jesus before the Sanhedrin. Again they had not mustered a representative body, but only a sprinkling of chief priests, scribes, and Elders. As Jesus was conducted across the courtyard, Peter shifted a little and saw him, battered and bruised, but still with such compassion in his eyes that Peter ran out of the house into the darkness, sobbing and ashamed. In spite of Jesus' warnings it had happened. He had slept and not prayed for strength. Temptation had come, and he had fallen headlong into it. Three times he had denied any knowledge of Jesus.

Someone else had been lurking about the High Priest's house during the hours of these examinations. It was Judas, who had seen too late what his betrayal had brought about, and that Jesus was condemned to death. No one knows what he had hoped for, but when he realized what he had done, he forced his way into the presence of the Chief Priests, flung down the thirty pieces of silver they had paid him, and cried, 'I have sinned! I have sinned! The man I betrayed was innocent.'

'That's nothing to do with us,' they replied, drawing away from him.

After a terrible silence he lurched out, and went and hanged himself.

The priests picked up the money – but it was blood money now, so they could not put it back in the treasury. They discussed what to do with it, and decided to buy a burial ground for aliens. Later they did so, and it became known as 'the field of blood'.

Jesus, still bound, was now brought before the Sanhedrin, and Caiaphas asked him again if he was the Christ. All the others who were present took up the question in a ragged, angry chorus of 'Are you the Son of God?'

'It is as you say,' Jesus replied.

'Then we need go no further,' they declared, and raised their hands in assent to the sentence of death.

The next step was to take the papers and the prisoner to Pilate, to get his signature and the execution order. In these papers they did not describe Jesus as guilty of blasphemy, but of sedition, of 'perverting' the people, and forbidding them to pay tribute to Rome; only later did they bring in that he had also called himself a King.

Pilate was in the Antonia Fortress, and Caiaphas would have been 'defiled' and unable to eat his Passover feast if he had gone under a Gentile roof at that time. He therefore begged Pilate to come out through the west gate to see him.

There Caiaphas and a few Elders waited with Jesus, still held by the Temple guards. It was early in the morning, between three and four, and Pilate wanted to settle the matter quickly and get indoors again.

'Well, what's the trouble?' he asked. 'What is the man accused of?'

When he found that what Caiaphas wanted was a death warrant with no evidence offered and no questions asked, he drew back.

'We should not have troubled you without satisfying ourselves that he was guilty of serious crimes,' Caiaphas told him stiffly.

'In that case, deal with him according to your own law,' Pilate replied.

'We are not permitted to carry out a death sentence,' Caiaphas pointed out. It was a sore point with the Jews.

Pilate saw then that he must examine Jesus himself, and for that purpose it was necessary for them to go inside the Fortress, to the Judgement Seat, while Caiaphas and the other Jews remained outside.

'Now,' Pilate began when he and Jesus faced one another. 'Are you a king?'

'Do you ask that for your own information?' Jesus replied. 'Or because it was stated in the charge?'

'Oh, I'm not a Jew!' Pilate exclaimed. 'But it is your own people who are accusing you. What did you do?'

'My kingdom is not of this world,' Jesus said. 'If it were, I should have men to fight for me so that I should not fall into enemy hands. But my kingdom is not of that kind.'

'You do call yourself a king then?' Pilate asked, rather baffled.

'That is your word,' Jesus said. 'I came into this world to bear witness to the truth. Everyone who understands the truth must recognize it in what I have taught.'

'Oh, truth!' exclaimed Pilate. 'What is truth?'

However, he found nothing to justify the sentence Caiaphas was asking, and he took Jesus back to him. People were already about, and knots of them lingered near the group of high Temple officials to see what was going on.

'I find no fault in him,' he said to Caiaphas, who was so enraged that he burst into an angry tirade about how Jesus had preached sedition all over the country, beginning down in Galilee and all the way through to Jerusalem.

'Galilee?' Pilate interrupted him, seeing a way out of his part of the business. 'Of course, he's a Galilean, and in that case he ought to go before Herod, not me.' He called to his men to take Jesus to the Palace by the Jaffa Gate where Herod had come to keep the Passover. It was right at the other side of the town, about half a mile away.

Herod appeared delighted to see him, and said he had long wanted to talk to him, and perhaps to see one of his miracles, and he began to ask questions on a variety of subjects, but Jesus answered none of them.

Caiaphas and the Elders had come with him, and seeing his silence they began to pour out their accusations. Still Jesus said nothing, and Herod shrugged his shoulders. It was really nothing to do with him. Jesus had committed no crime meriting death on his territory, and he turned him over to his soldiers and allowed them to do what they liked with him before sending him back to Pilate. Herod's men mocked him, and dressed him up in a purple robe as he called himself a king, and so he was taken back to the Antonia, over that half mile of public road.

Pilate was getting uneasy and very impatient. He did not care what happened to Jesus, but the Jews were a difficult people to handle in matters of their religion and he did not want to incur censure from the Emperor for his handling of the situation. In spite of having found no fault in him, and though he had felt Jesus' power and authority, Pilate now said to Caiaphas,

'I find no grounds for the accusations you make against this man, nor has Herod. I'll scourge him and release him, since it is the custom for us to release a prisoner at the Passover.'

Caiaphas had not expected that, but he was ready for it, and asked instead for the release of a man who was lying under sentence of death for sedition. He had worked against Rome for a long time, had killed more than one Roman, and was something of a national hero in consequence. He was therefore a good man to put up for the Passover release as a rival to Jesus who had claimed to be the Messiah but showed neither the power nor the desire to overthrow Rome.

So the High Priest said, 'We want Barabbas as the prisoner released to us for the Passover.' And he shouted *'Barabbas!'* loudly for the gathering crowds to hear.

Before Pilate had come down to the Jews this time, his wife had sent him a note which said, 'Have nothing to do with this case. The man is innocent, and I have dreamed terrible things this night on his account.'

Pilate suddenly remembered those words as he stood facing Jesus' enemies. The crowd, inspired by Caiaphas, began to shout for Jesus to be crucified.

'Stop!' Pilate's voice rang out. 'What harm has he done?'

But the crowd only yelled, 'Barabbas! Barabbas! Barabbas!' and 'Crucify him!'

He took Jesus back again to the Judgement Seat, set up on the vast Pavement within the Fortress. Though he considered him innocent, he ordered the lash to be administered, and handed him over to the Roman soldiers, who entered into the

The Antonia Fortress

task as though it was one of their games. Indeed, it may have been just that, for excavation of the Pavement has revealed a record of soldiers' games which have been found also on other Roman sites – varieties of hop-scotch, knucklebones, mazes, with their appropriate emblems, diagrams or frames scratched into the stone as with the point of a sword.

But there was also 'the game of the king', with a crown of thorns as its emblem, in which the victim was dressed and set up as King, mocked, tortured and killed.

So, after they had scourged Jesus they gave him back the robe of royal purple, plaited thorns to be his crown, and gave him a reed for sceptre. They knelt before him in derision, rising quickly from their knees to hit him in the face as they cried, 'Hail, King of the Jews!'

So it was that Pilate brought him again to the High Priests at the gateway into the city, and showed him, battered as he was, to the crowds which had gathered there, saying,

'*Ecce homo!* Behold the man. I find no fault in him.'

'He blasphemed.' Caiaphas now spat out the charge he had tried to hide from Rome. 'He said he was the Son of God. Therefore, by our Law, he ought to die.'

Pilate, a Roman with a host of gods and goddesses, heard those words with a shiver of superstitious dread. Was this what his wife's warning had meant?

He went back to question Jesus once more – Jesus, as the son of a god.

'What are you?' he asked uneasily, but Jesus made no reply.

'Don't you realize that I have power to crucify you, or to set you free?' he persisted with rising anger.

'You could have no power over me unless it was given you from above,' Jesus replied. 'The sin rests on those who handed me over to you.'

Even Pilate held his power by the will of God, but he was ignorant, and Jesus had taught plainly that those who were ignorant were not guilty of sin. But Caiaphas was God's own representative among His chosen people. He should have known the words of God, and the will of God. But he had said in effect, 'No matter whether you find him innocent or not, we want him killed.'

Nervous now and uncertain of himself, Pilate tried again

to persuade the High Priests to let Jesus go, but they cried, 'You are a traitor to Caesar if you set him free!'

He then showed Jesus again to the crowd, and said, 'Behold your King.'

'Away with him!' they cried. 'Crucify him!'

'Shall I really crucify your King?' he asked Caiaphas.

'We have no king but Caesar,' the High Priest replied – and no one in the crowd protested.

The noise was terrific, and Pilate yielded. But he brought out water and washed his hands ceremoniously before them all, to show the world that the responsibility was not his.

'See you to it,' he said.

'His blood be on us and on our children,' promised the priests.

CHAPTER 27

IT IS FINISHED

JESUS was given back his own clothes before he was led away to execution. Pilate returned him to the Jews, but Roman soldiers were in charge of the carrying out of the sentence, which was to take place on a low mound outside the north wall, for the Holy City must not be defiled with blood. Two thieves were to be executed at the same time, both by crucifixion, and each carried his cross from the Antonia to the place which was called Golgotha.

Jesus was exhausted by all he had had to endure since that last meal with the Twelve, and after he had gone a little way he sank down under the weight of the cross. An African from Libya happened to be passing by, and was called over to carry it for him, and became, even at that late hour, a faithful disciple. The grim procession was watched by many people, women among them, who wailed in lamentation for his fate, but Jesus, turning his eyes upon them, said:

'Weep not for me, ye daughters of Jerusalem, but for yourselves and your children.'

Each cross had to bear on it a notice authorized by Pilate stating the grounds upon which the death sentence had been passed. For Jesus he wrote:

'This is Jesus of Nazareth, the King of the Jews.'

Caiaphas protested when he saw it and demanded that it should be altered at least to, 'He called himself King of the Jews'. But Pilate had been through something himself that day, and what he had seen of them had only intensified his contempt for the Jews.

'What I have written, I have written,' he replied.

'Weep not for me, ye daughters of Jerusalem, but for yourselves'

Stripped of his garments, Jesus was nailed to the cross through hands and feet, and while the soldiers carried out their task he was heard to pray:

'Father, forgive them. They know not what they do.'

187

The cross was raised up, to stand between those on which the thieves hung. The soldiers brought the customary drink of wine with myrrh in it to deaden the pain, but Jesus would not drink it. He had gone willingly, with his eyes open, into all that had happened, and he would not now allow any moment of it to escape him.

It was still only about nine in the morning. Four Roman soldiers were detailed to stay and see it through. They had no great concern about it. It was simply their job, and they were accustomed to such sights. They despised the Jews anyway. The prisoners' clothes became theirs, and they shared them out, but when they came to the long cassock-like garment Jesus had worn, they found it had been woven and shaped in one piece. There were no seams to rip up, and cut into four parts it would not have been worth anything. They therefore tossed for it.

Even at Golgotha there were crowds, they hissed and booed. The soldiers taunted Jesus and shouted, 'Save yourself, if you're the King of the Jews!'

Men in the crowd yelled, 'You who were going to destroy the Temple and build it up again in three days, save yourself, if you can, and come down from that cross!' And they guffawed at their wit.

One of the thieves hanging beside him interrupted his own swearing and cursing to say savagely, 'If you're Christ, save us, can't you, and yourself!' But the other reproved him and asked, 'Aren't you afraid! We're all three in the same boat, but you and I are getting what we deserved. He's done no wrong!' And he said to Jesus, 'Master, remember me when you come into your Kingdom.'

'I will,' Jesus promised. 'Today you shall be with me in Paradise.'

He looked down then on a little group standing together at the foot of the cross. His mother was there, and John with his mother, and Mary, the sister of Martha.

Jesus said to his mother, 'John will be your son now.'

And to John he said: 'Behold, your mother,' and John put his arm round her, and led her away so that she should not see the worst of her son's agony. Thereafter he looked after her as if she were in fact his own mother.

The chief Priests and Elders made another group, smiling and cynical.

'He was great at saving others,' they said, 'evidently he cannot save himself. If he really is the King of Israel, chosen of God, let us see him come down from the cross and we might yet believe in him!'

A shadow seemed to fall across the sun when Jesus had hung there for about three hours, and it was dark for a long time, or so it seemed to those who watched the Master dying. For him too it was a time of darkness, of great suffering both in body and soul. The words of the 22nd Psalm must have been in his mind, for presently he cried out in the tongue of his boyhood, the opening sentence, '*Eloi, Eloi, Lama sabachthani?*' – 'My God, My God, why has thou forsaken me?' It continues with the words, '*Why art thou so far from helping me? All that see me, laugh me to scorn; Be not far from me, for trouble is near, and there is none to help. I am poured out like water, and all my bones are sundered. My strength is dried up, and my tongue cleaveth to my jaws. Thou hast brought me into the dust of death. But be not far from me, O Lord. O my strength, haste Thee to help me.*'

But in that darkest hour there came to him assurance that what he had found had been truly God's will. Faith and courage shone through him. He was no victim, no passive lamb borne to the slaughter. Not one second of his trials had been in vain, all tended towards the accomplishment of the purpose of God. Being thus so strangely lifted up, he did indeed draw all men to him. Somehow this terrible-seeming end was only the beginning. By foreseeing, guiding and deliberately accepting this sacrifice of all his human life, his body and his

suffering, he had triumphed miraculously – God through him had triumphed miraculously.

'I thirst,' he murmured in the extremity of weakness, and the soldiers handed up a sponge dipped in their ration of sour wine on the tip of a javelin.

Jesus moistened his dry mouth, and gave a loud cry.

'It is finished,' he was heard to say.

All was accomplished.

Then, content, with almost his last breath he repeated the prayer his mother had taught him as a small boy, and which he had said ever since when he lay down to sleep.

'Father, into Thy hands I commend my spirit.'

His head sank on to his shoulder, and he was dead.

The centurion who was in charge of the soldiers was standing at that moment close to the foot of the middle cross, and when he heard Jesus' words and saw what had happened, he exclaimed, 'This man was indeed the Son of God!'

The Romans usually left bodies hanging until they disintegrated, but Jewish Law ordered that they must be disposed of before sundown, so this being the day of the Passover Feast, Caiaphas went to Pilate and asked him to order the soldiers to break the legs of the three men to hasten their deaths. Pilate agreed, but Jesus was dead before the soldiers brought along their mallets. Nevertheless, they stabbed him in the side with a spear to make sure.

Caiaphas had very little time left before going to celebrate that feast which was the holiest in the whole Jewish calendar. Very soon he and the Elders, the Pharisees and the Rabbis, would be eating the Paschal lamb, and passing round the cups of wine. Father to son and son to father, they would be reciting again the story of their great deliverance from slavery, they would bless the name of the Lord, and sing the Great Hallel, as Jesus and his Apostles had sung it so short a time ago, in the upper room.

In the meantime, a rich member of the Sanhedrin, a good man called Joseph of Arimathea, went as soon as he saw Jesus was dead to ask Pilate if he might bury the body. Pilate readily made him a present of it, but on second thoughts he sent for the centurion from the scene of the crucifixions to come and report on the matter. The man confirmed that Jesus was dead before Pilate's message had arrived.

Nicodemus, that timid member of the Sanhedrin, accompanied Joseph and brought with him a load of myrrh and aloes to embalm the body. Joseph had laid linen ready in the new tomb he had bought close by. Together they lifted Jesus' body down, and carried it thither. There was not time before sundown to care for it properly, as they were bound to observe the Law and be back in their own homes by six o'clock, as for a Sabbath. They sprinkled the body thickly with spices, bound the strips of linen about it, fastened a napkin about the head, and rested the body carefully on the new stone slab. Then they rolled the flat millstone across the entrance and went away.

Mary of Bethany and two other women had followed them to the tomb, and remained beside it weeping after Joseph and Nicodemus had gone away.

CHAPTER 28

THE THIRD DAY

JESUS' death on the cross was hard to accept, even by those nearest to him. To Gentiles – the Romans and other non-believers – it was simple nonsense to think of worshipping a man who had died on the gallows at the hands of his own people. To many Jews it was final proof that Jesus was not and could not be the Messiah.

Of the eleven Apostles only John, whom Jesus loved most dearly, had been brave enough to follow him all through the ordeal of that night. He had been absent only while he took Mary and his own mother away to the house of friends. After that he remained at the foot of the cross until the end. Yet even he had run away in the first shock of the arrest in the Garden.

Peter's world was upside down. He was angry and disturbed. He had pinned his faith to the belief that Jesus had power to change the world. For that he had thrown aside his old life, his home and family, even his skill as a fisherman. He understood that men might plot against Jesus, but he had been passionately sure that they could never prevail. Now, the arrest and the trials with all their terrible malice, the mockery and lies, ending in the triumph of the Temple and the Chief Priests, crashed through all he had hoped and believed, and left him wildly disturbed, not knowing which way to turn.

He had seen Lazarus brought back from the dead, and the five thousand fed – but what did they mean, with Jesus dead on the cross? Where was his power? Where was God Himself?

Peter was angry, frightened, and desperately ashamed, with no one to turn to, and no hope left.

If only Jesus had stepped down from the cross, how many might have been convinced and converted!

Christ crucified remained for long afterwards a terrible stumbling-block to those who had believed in him.

But John had known at least that the warnings Jesus had given his disciples to fortify them for what happened were all-important and somehow explained all. He understood that stepping down from the cross would have been dangerously like that temptation in the wilderness, tempting God by throwing himself down from the topmost pinnacle of the Temple. John had already a glimmer of understanding that somehow every slow second of that night, the whole agonizing ordeal from the supper they had eaten together right on to the end, was teeming with meaning if they could only see it, and pregnant with the purposes of God.

But Peter could neither talk nor listen. The turmoil within him was too great. He was no 'rock'. He had no strength, no help, no understanding to offer to the others who were also suffering. He only wished he could die.

It was John who went after him and brought him back into the company of the Eleven. John was the disciple Jesus loved, but Peter had been his right-hand man, and his strength was needed now, for fear lay over the other disciples, fear that the Elders would seek them out and kill them also. They had shut themselves in and barred their doors and dared not go out again. Over that Sabbath which followed Jesus' death none of them remembered that he had said he would rise again. None of them tried to find him. None of them went to Galilee as he had told them. He was dead and gone.

But very early next morning, on the first day of the week, Mary of Bethany and two other women went out before it was light to anoint the dead body. They carried spices with them and Mary's broken flask of precious ointment. As they hurried along, to the place outside the city walls, Mary remembered the stone Joseph and Nicodemus had rolled over the entrance to the grave, and wondered whether they would be able to move it alone. She wished they had brought some of the men with them.

Then, when they were near enough, they saw that the stone was no longer in position. A gaping hole in the rock brought them up short.

'Supposing someone has removed his body!' Mary thought, and ran back to find Peter and John. It was Peter she found first and, still blind with grief, he blundered off at once towards Golgotha. Then she found John, and he outran Peter and reached the tomb first. He did not go inside, but stooped and peered in, and saw the white linens lying on the burial slab, but no body was there. Peter arrived panting, and pushed past him, going right inside the cave. He did not touch anything, only stared, for the linen cloths lay in their coils, collapsed, as though the body had slipped from between them without disturbing so much as a thread, or a fold of the linen. The napkin was there too, the length of a neck from the other cloth, with a strip of bare rock showing between.

After a moment John went in and stood beside Peter. John understood at least that Jesus had risen, but Peter was still too deep in his misery to think. His eyes saw dimly and his mind was numb. John nudged him gently out of the place and they went home, leaving Mary weeping outside the empty tomb.

For a time she lingered, mourning, then a memory of John's and Peter's faces pierced her grief, and she went to look for herself at what they had seen. She did not notice the linen. What she found there were two angels, one where Jesus' head had rested, one where his feet had been.

If God was there, the crucifixion could not be the end. Then the angels spoke kindly to her, asking why she wept. At that, her first dismay returned. His body had been taken away! She drifted out again, weeping more bitterly, looking

helplessly round, and saw someone standing near the entrance. She did not look particularly at him but thought he might be a gardener, perhaps in charge of the burial ground.

'Why are you crying so?' he asked her. 'Who are you looking for?'

'Oh sir, if it was you who moved him,' she replied quickly, 'let me know where he is and I will take him away.'

Then she heard her name spoken, in a voice she knew.

'Master!' she cried, and fell on her knees to bathe his feet again with her tears, to draw together the broken flesh. But Jesus stepped back.

'Do not cling to me,' he said gently, 'for I have not yet returned to the Father. But go back and tell my Brothers that I am risen. Say to them that I will go on to Galilee and await them there.'

By 'Brothers' he referred to the Apostles, and Mary ran to find them, crying breathlessly, 'I have seen the Lord!'

They did not believe her, and they did not go to Galilee. The disappearance of Jesus' body was a fresh source of fear, for the disciples might be accused of stealing it.

That afternoon two of the later disciples, not of the original twelve, walked out from Jerusalem to a village about seven miles away called Emmaus, talking all the way of the crucifixion and the empty tomb and the story Mary had brought back. A man fell quietly into step beside them, and asked what they were discussing. They glanced at him in surprise.

'There must be few people in Jerusalem today,' they replied, 'who don't know what has happened there.'

'Tell me about it,' the man said.

'Why – Jesus of Nazareth, a very great prophet,' they replied, 'was condemned to death by the High Priests and crucified.'

'We had great hopes that he was going to redeem Israel,' the other added, 'but this is the third day since his death.'

'Some women went to his tomb early this morning,' the first took up the story, 'and his body was not there. They said they saw angels who said he was alive.'

'Foolish ones,' said the stranger, 'so slow to believe what the prophets have told you.' And he began to show them how Christ's coming had been promised from the beginning of time, through Moses and all the prophets.

They had reached the village by then, and the disciples asked him to stay longer with them as dusk was coming down, but they had not recognized him. They went in together to a house and a meal was brought for them. Then the stranger took up the bread and blessed it and passed it to them – and that little familiar touch showed them who it was. But as soon as they recognized him he was gone. With the bread still in their hands, one said to the other, 'I felt as though my heart would burst while he was talking.' The other nodded. 'I never understood the Scriptures like that before.'

They left the meal and went headlong back to Jerusalem to tell what they had seen. The door was unlocked to admit them, and locked quickly behind them. The two from Emmaus began to say. 'The Master is really risen!' – when some of the others chimed in with – 'He is indeed. Simon Peter has seen him.'

The next moment Jesus was in the room with them saying, 'Peace be with you' – and many of them were afraid, thinking they were shut in a room with a ghost.

But Jesus said, 'See ... my hands, my feet. Is it not me, myself? Handle me and be sure. Has a ghost flesh and bones? See for yourselves that I have.' Then, as though to lighten the atmosphere, he asked, 'Have you anything to eat?'

Joy crept round the room as their eyes rested on him, and Jesus said again, 'Peace be with you! As the Father sent me into this world, I send you forth. Come close,' and as they clustered about him he breathed upon them as though handing on to them the very breath out of his own body. 'Receive ye the spirit,' he said. 'From henceforth, if any of you forgives sins, forgiven they will be. If any of you binds a man's sins on him, bound they will remain.'

It happened that Thomas was not present that night, and when he heard what had happened he could not believe it. They described how Jesus had held out his scarred hands for them to see, and his feet, but Thomas's doubts remained. Common sense was all against it.

'Unless I can touch them myself, I shan't believe it,' he declared.

A week later, Jesus came again among them, and this time Thomas was there.

'Thomas,' Jesus called, 'stretch out your finger and feel my hands. Put your hand under my garments and feel my side. Come believing, not thinking it impossible.'

Looking at him, Thomas made no move to stretch out a hand to feel those scars.

'My Lord and my God,' he said slowly, with adoration.

'Is it only because you see me that you believe?' Jesus asked, but his tone showed that he knew it was not so. 'Blessed are they who do not see, yet believe.'

A little while after this the disciples went over the familiar hills to Galilee. Simon Peter and John, James and probably Andrew, Thomas and Nathanael walked together round the lake. Peter was emerging from his wretched state, though there was still a shadow between him and the risen Lord. Presently, with a touch of his old impetuosity, he said, 'I'm going fishing.'

'All right,' the others agreed. 'We'll come too.'

They took a biggish boat which had a little one in tow. It was dark as they rowed over the waters. Peter, glorying in his old skill, threw off his clothes and worked naked. They cast their nets again and again all through the night but caught nothing. Then in the early light Jesus stood on the shore and hailed them.

'Hallo!' he called. 'You haven't caught anything, have you?'

'No!' they called back, not recognizing him.

'Cast your net in on the right side of the boat and you'll find plenty.'

They did so, and this time fish swarmed into it. It was so heavy they could not raise it.

John, always a step in front of the others, had been watching the figure on the shore and now said to Peter, 'It's the Master.'

Peter, hastily pulling his coat about him, plunged into the water. Some of the others climbed into the little boat and rowed to shore, trailing the heavy net behind them. As they beached the boat they saw that Jesus had a fish cooking over a small fire and that there was some bread at hand.

'Bring some of your fish,' he called, and Peter went back for them. He counted what was in the net – and there were one hundred and fifty-three large fish.

'Come and eat,' Jesus said, and there was a feeling of awe on them all, for they knew who he was. Jesus handed them bread and fish, and they ate.

When they had all finished, Jesus said:

'Simon' – not using the name he had given him, 'Peter', his 'rock'. 'Do you love me more than any of these others?'

No one had forgotten how earnestly Peter had declared that night in the upper room, after the Passover supper,

'Come and eat'

'Master, though everyone else falter, I never will,' and 'Even if it meant dying with you, I would not deny you.' They all knew too what the sequel had been.

Peter also remembered. He no longer claimed to love Jesus more than anyone else, but answered humbly, 'I love you dearly, Master.'

'Feed my lambs,' Jesus said, thus taking him back into service as one of his shepherds.

Then Jesus spoke to him again, and asked, 'Simon, do you love me truly?'

'You know I love you dearly, Master,' Peter replied unhappily.

'Feed my sheep,' said Jesus.

A third time Jesus asked his question, once for each of Peter's denials. This time he used Peter's own phrase. 'Simon, do you love me dearly?'

Deeply distressed, Simon replied pleadingly, 'Master, you know all there is in my heart. You know that I love you dearly.'

Then all was forgiven, the betrayal was wiped out, and Peter was reinstated, back in his place as right-hand man.

'Feed my sheep,' Jesus said.

After that, since all was known and forgiven, Jesus spoke to him from the heart, knowing what the years would bring him, the long life which lay ahead, the death he was to die.

'When you were young,' he said, 'you dressed yourself and walked where you pleased: but you will grow old. Then you will stretch out your hands and another will clothe you, and take you where you will not wish to go.'

Peter accepted gratefully what he understood, that there were years of service ahead, and the other thing, which he could not fully comprehend, which was that he too would die upon a cross.

Earlier Jesus had said, 'You cannot follow where I am going, Peter.' Now the position had changed. Jesus' physical presence was soon to be withdrawn, and his final words to Peter were, 'You will follow me.'

Restored and redeemed, Peter was himself again, and a moment later as his eyes rested on John, the old lively spirit asserted itself, and he cried impulsively.

'What about John, Master? What will happen to him?'

It brought rebuke. 'If it is my wish that he should stay till I come, that is not your affair,' Jesus replied. 'You follow me.'

Because of those words people began to think that John would never die – though that was not what Jesus had said, or meant, and this was carefully recorded in the Gospel of St John where the incident is told. But John was the only one of the Apostles who died a natural death. He lived on for many years after Jerusalem had been destroyed and, as Jesus had foretold, not one stone of Herod's Temple was left standing.

CHAPTER 29

BEHOLD I AM WITH YOU ALWAYS

AT various times during a period of forty days, Jesus was seen in his risen state, sometimes by one or two together, once by a gathering of five hundred people. There were plenty of them still alive to recall the fact when these things came to be written down.

After the breakfast with Jesus on the shores of the lake, the Apostles remained a few days longer in Galilee. Then he told them to go bravely back to Jerusalem, to wait there for the power which the Father had promised, through him, to come upon them.

'John baptized you all with water,' he reminded them. 'Now before many days you will receive that other baptism of fire and Holy Spirit.'

This he had revealed long ago to Nicodemus, when he said also that a man has to be born again before he can enter the kingdom.

'What is born of flesh is flesh,' he had said, 'but spirit is born only of spirit . . . and spirit is like the wind blowing over the desert.'

He told them again that they were his witnesses who had heard his words and seen his works. On them he relied for the spreading of the light to the whole world, first in Jerusalem, then throughout Israel, and so to the ends of the earth.

One last journey he took them along the road to Bethany, and on the Mount of Olives, looking back over the stones of Jerusalem, he blessed them and left them. Angels received him and bore him hence, leaving in their hearts his promise,

'Behold, I am with you always, unto the end of the world.'

CHAPTER 30

KNOW ALL YE WHO LISTEN

THE story is nearly told.

There was no more hiding behind locked doors, no more fear and distrust, among those Jesus had left behind. Peter was strong again. He was the rock on which a house could safely be built. He took his place as leader among them.

Ten days after Jesus had left them on the Mount of Olives and returned to the Father, the Feast of Pentecost came round. In the Jewish calendar it was a day of thanksgiving for the First Fruits of the Harvest, and it was on that day that the promised baptism of 'fire and Holy Spirit' came to the Twelve. (The Eleven had chosen another to replace Judas in their company.) They were sitting in what was probably the room in which they had eaten the last supper with Jesus.

Suddenly a great wind blew through the house, and into the room where they were. Tongues of flame danced in it and settled on each of them. Strange words came to their lips, and they rushed out into the streets to speak them. Many foreigners in the city heard them and understood as though they had been spoken to in their own language.

There was tremendous excitement among them all, but scoffers pointed at the Apostles and said they had been drinking. Peter rallied the others round him, and spoke plainly for all to hear.

'Know, all ye who listen,' he cried. 'These men are not drunk, for it is still early morning. No, this is the day long promised by the prophet Joel . . . the great day when the Holy Spirit is poured out on all men. The day when your sons and

Peter was strong again.

daughters may prophesy, your old men dream dreams, and your young men see visions.

'Men of Israel, hearken! For Jesus of Nazareth, whom you killed, God has raised up. And He has made that same Jesus both Lord and Christ. To that we all are witnesses. So repent and be baptized, every one of you, in the name of Jesus Christ, that your sins may be forgiven, and you too may receive the gift of the Spirit.'

Also in Puffin

THE *PARENTS* BOOK OF BEDTIME STORIES

Edited by Tony Bradman

Bedtime will always be a pleasure with this refreshing book of bedtime stories drawn from the popular *Parents* magazine. With plenty of lively and appealing characters and a wide range of themes (and all the perfect length for a bedtime slot), this is an ideal addition to the family bookshelf.

ANOTHER BIG STORY BOOK

ed. Richard Bamberger

One of the foremost experts on literature for children has collected here some of the world's most enchanting and magical fairy-tales. From the English tale 'Jack and the Beanstalk' to the Indian 'Wali Dad the Simple', these are stories parents will enjoy telling and children will remember with pleasure for the rest of their lives.

BAD BOYS

ed. Eileen Colwell

All the boys in these twelve stories are bad in one way or another. Either really bad, like Freddie, Adolphus, Edward, Montague, Montmorency and John Henry, who leave their aunts marooned on an island, or only a little bad, like Timothy, who jumps in and out of puddles.